Working Together or Apart: Promoting the Next Generation of Digital Scholarship

Report of a Workshop Cosponsored by
the Council on Library and Information Resources and
The National Endowment for the Humanities

March 2009

Council on Library and Information Resources
Washington, D.C.

ISBN 978-1-932326-33-8
CLIR Publication No. 145
Published by:

Council on Library and Information Resources
1752 N Street NW, Suite 800
Washington, DC 20036
Web site at http://www.clir.org

Additional copies are available for $25 each. Orders must be placed through CLIR's Web site.
This publication is also available online at no charge at http://www.clir.org/pubs/abstract/pub145abst.html.

The paper in this publication meets the minimum requirements of the American National Standard for Information Sciences—Permanence of Paper for Printed Library Materials ANSI Z39.48-1984.

Cover image: Digital recreation of the space of the Amiens Cathedral nave, from "Amiens II," Columbia University.
Image courtesy of Stephen Murray.

Library of Congress Cataloging-in-Publication Data

Working together or apart : promoting the next generation of digital scholarship : report of a workshop cosponsored by the Council on Library and Information Resources and the National Endowment for the Humanities.
p. cm. -- (CLIR publication ; no. 145)
Includes bibliographical references.
ISBN 978-1-932326-33-8 (alk. paper)
1. Communication in learning and scholarship--Technological innovations. 2. Information technology. 3. Learning and scholarship--Social aspects. 4. Scholarly electronic publishing. I. Council on Library and Information Resources. II. National Endowment for the Humanities. III. Title. IV. Series.

AZ195.W675 2009
001.2--dc22

2009010911

Contents

About the Authors iv
Acknowledgments vii

Asking Questions and Building a Research Agenda for Digital Scholarship, by Amy Friedlander 1

Tools for Thinking: ePhilology and Cyberinfrastructure, by Gregory Crane, Alison Babeu, David Bamman, Lisa Cerrato, Rashmi Singhal. 16

The Changing Landscape of American Studies in a Global Era, by Caroline Levander 27

A Whirlwind Tour of Automated Language Processing for the Humanities and Social Sciences, by Douglas W. Oard 34

Information Visualization: Challenge for the Humanities, by Maureen Stone 43

Art History and the New Media: Representation and the Production of Humanistic Knowledge, by Stephen Murray 57

Social Attention in the Age of the Web, by Bernardo A. Huberman 62

Digital Humanities Centers: Loci for Digital Scholarship, by Diane M. Zorich 70

About the Authors

Alison Babeu has served as the digital librarian and research coordinator for the Perseus Project since 2004. Before coming to Perseus, she worked as a librarian at both the Harvard Business School and the Boston Public Library. She has a B.A. in History from Mount Holyoke College and an M.L.S. from Simmons College.

David Bamman is a senior researcher in computational linguistics for the Perseus Project, focusing on natural language processing for Latin and Greek, including treebank construction, computational lexicography, morphological tagging, and word sense disambiguation. He received a B.A. in Classics from the University of Wisconsin-Madison and an M.A. in Applied Linguistics from Boston University. He is currently leading the development of the Dynamic Lexicon Project and the Latin and Ancient Greek Dependency Treebanks.

Lisa Cerrato is managing editor of the Perseus Project, overseeing a variety of work. She received a B.A. in Latin from Tufts University and has been with the project since 1994. Her interests include furthering classical education, particularly Latin and Greek, teaching with technology, and user-driven content management.

Gregory Crane is professor of Classics at Tufts University. His research interests are twofold. He has published on a wide range of ancient Greek authors (including books on Homer and Thucydides). At the same time, he has a long-standing interest in the relationship between the humanities and rapidly developing digital technology. He began this side of his work as a graduate student at Harvard when the Classics Department purchased its first TLG authors on magnetic tape in the summer of 1982, and he has worked continuously on aspects of digital humanities ever since. His current research focuses on what a cyberinfrastructure for the humanities in general and classics in particular would look like. He is especially interested in how technology can extend the intellectual range of researchers moving through very large collections and working with more languages than was ever possible in print culture.

Amy Friedlander is director of programs at the Council on Library and Information Resources where she is primarily engaged in projects involving cyberinfrastructure, preservation, and digital scholarship, encouraging partnerships and cross-fertilization of ideas across disciplines, agencies, and institutional boundaries. She is the founding editor of *D-Lib Magazine* and subsequently SAIC's now-defunct *iMP: The magazine on information impacts*. She has also participated in the organizational phases of the Library of Congress' National Digital Information Infrastructure and Preservation Program. Since joining CLIR in 2007, Ms. Friedlander has been appointed to the National Science Foundation's Blue Ribbon Task Force on Economically Sustainable Digital Preservation and Access, guest-edited a special issue of the *Journal of Electronic Publishing* on communication and cyberinfrastructure, and organized a workshop with Gregory Crane on the implications of large-scale text digital corpora for humanities scholarship. She is the author of five short monographs on the history of large-scale, technology-based infrastructures in the United States.

Bernardo A. Huberman is a senior HP fellow and the director of the Information Dynamics Lab at Hewlett Packard Laboratories. He is also a consulting professor in the Department of Applied Physics at Stanford University. For the past eight years his research has concentrated on the phenomenon of the Web, with an emphasis on understanding its implications for social dynamics and the design of novel mechanisms for discovering and aggregating information. He is the author the book, *The Laws of the Web: Patterns in the Ecology of Information*, published by MIT Press.

Caroline Levander is professor of English and director of the Humanities Research Center at Rice University. She is currently writing *Laying Claim: Imagining Empire on the U.S. Mexico Border* (under contract, Oxford University Press) and *The Idea of American Literature* (for Wiley-Blackwell's Manifesto Series), and is co-editing *Engaging the Americas* (Palgrave Macmillan). She is author of *Cradle of Liberty: Race, the Child and National Belonging from Thomas Jefferson to W.E.B. Du Bois* (Duke University Press, 2006) and *Voices of the Nation: Women and Public Speech in Nineteenth-Century American Culture and Literature* (Cambridge University Press, 1998) as well as co-editor of *Hemispheric American Studies* (Rutgers University Press, 2008) and *The American Child: A Cultural Studies Reader* (Rutgers University Press, 2003).

Stephen Murray is professor of art history and archaeology at Columbia University. In his research and publications he has explored the life of the great Gothic cathedrals of France (Notre-Dame of Paris, Amiens, Beauvais and Troyes). He believes that it is important to consider all aspects of the cathedral including design, construction, social context, and liturgical function: this inclusive agenda inspired his most recent book, *A Gothic Sermon* (University of California Press, 2004). To animate the cathedral and to make it available to as wide an audience as possible he has, most recently, experimented with the digital media, including the Internet, three-dimensional computer modeling, and video. Mr. Murray was educated at Oxford and London Universities. He has held grants and fellowships from the Guggenheim Foundation, the Stanford Center for Advanced Studies in the Behavioral Sciences, the National Humanities Center, the National Endowment for the Humanities, and The Andrew W. Mellon Foundation. He was founding director of the Media Center for Art History at Columbia.

Douglas W. Oard is associate dean for research at the University of Maryland's College of Information Studies. He holds joint appointments as an associate professor in the College of Information Studies and the Institute for Advanced Computing Studies. His research is focused on the design and evaluation of interactive systems to support search and sense-making in large collections of character-coded, scanned, and spoken language. He is best known for his work on cross-language information retrieval, but his current interests also include support for e-discovery in litigation (as a coordinator for the TREC Legal Track) and investigating the application of computational linguistics for social science research (as a co-PI for the NSF-funded PopIT Human Social Dynamics project). He earned his Ph.D. in Electrical Engineering from the University of Maryland, College Park, and a Master of Electrical Engineering degree from Rice University.

Rashmi Singhal is lead programmer at the Perseus Project. She received a B.S. in Computer Science and Archaeology from Tufts University and is primarily interested in the applications of computer technology in archaeology.

Maureen Stone, founder of StoneSoup Consulting, has worked in digital color, graphics, perception, and the tools for information display for almost 30 years. At Xerox PARC in the 1980s, she participated in the desktop publishing revolution, creating tools for illustration, typography, and color selection. She and her colleagues created some of the first color management systems for digital prepress, uniquely focused on purely digital imagery (as opposed to scanned photographs). At the end of her tenure at PARC, she was a member of RED (Research in Experimental Design), a small group exploring the relationship between technology and design, where she worked on digital sound, 3D Web graphics, and a walk-through comic strip. Since founding StoneSoup Consulting in 1999, she has worked on a wide range of research and development activities, from building multi-projector display walls at Stanford to designing color palettes for Tableau Software to teaching Information Visualization in the University of Washington iSchool. She is an adjunct professor at Simon Fraser University's School for Interactive Arts and Technology, and editor in chief of *IEEE Computer Graphics & Applications*. Her book, *A Field Guide to Digital Color*, was published by A. K. Peters in 2003.

Diane M. Zorich is a cultural heritage consultant specializing in planning and managing the delivery of cultural information. Her clients include the J. Paul Getty Trust, the American Association of Museums, the Smithsonian Institution, RLG Programs / OCLC, and many other cultural organizations and institutions. Before establishing her consultancy, Ms. Zorich was data manager at the Association of Systematics Collections, and documentation manager at the Peabody Museum of Archaeology and Ethnology at Harvard University. She served as past president and Board member of the Museum Computer Network, and was chair of that organization's Intellectual Property Special Interest Group. She is the author of *Introduction to Managing Digital Assets: Options for Cultural and Education Organizations* (J. Paul Getty Trust, 1999), *Developing Intellectual Property Policies: A "How-To" Guide for Museums* (Canadian Heritage Information Network, 2003), and *A Survey of Digital Humanities Centers in the United States* (Council on Library and Information Resources, 2008).

Acknowledgments

The Council on Library and Information Resources (CLIR) is grateful to the National Endowment for the Humanities (NEH) for its cosponsorship of the workshop for Promoting Digital Scholarship on September 15, 2008, and subsequent publication through Cooperative Agreements HC-50002-08 and HC-50004-08. Special thanks are due to Brett Bobley and Joel Wurl at NEH for their guidance and support throughout the planning process. CLIR is also indebted to Stephen Griffin and Lucille Nowell of the National Science Foundation; Clifford Lynch of the Coalition for Networked Information; Joyce Ray of the Institute for Museum and Library Services; and Donald Waters of The Andrew W. Mellon Foundation for their contributions to the steering committee. Finally, CLIR would like to thank the authors of the papers in this volume and participants in the September 2008 workshop, as well as those who came to an earlier workshop on November 28, 2007. These discussions have enriched this publication.

Amy Friedlander was the project director, Kathlin Smith and Brian Leney edited, designed and produced this report.

"Men work together," I told him from the heart,
"Whether they work together or apart."

(From *Tuft of Flowers*, by Robert Frost)

Asking Questions and Building a Research Agenda for Digital Scholarship

Amy Friedlander

At a critical moment in the movie *The Unbearable Lightness of Being*,[1] the audience sees a glass tremble on a table. Because the story is set in Prague Spring of 1968, we know the rattling glass and then the faint rumble signal the arrival of Soviet tanks. But the tremors go unnoticed by the characters, Tomas, played by Daniel Day-Lewis, and Tereza, played by Juliette Binoche, who are arguing over their disintegrating relationship. She decides to leave him, steps out into the street, and realizes that there has been an invasion.

In this scene, the director Philip Kaufman has engaged in an elegant bit of storytelling that takes advantage both of the audience's knowledge, which exceeds that of the characters, and the attributes of the medium. He uses film, photography, and sound to fill in the story around the narrative conveyed by the script to evoke apprehensive, emotional responses from the audience precisely because they are more knowledgeable than the characters. It is similar to the poignancy that accompanies a good production of *Romeo and Juliet*. Yes, we know it will not end well, but somehow every time, we root for the lovers. In the case of this film, the audience's foreknowledge is triggered by adroit use of the camera and the medium rather than by familiarity with the story.

So it is with computation and humanities scholarship. We have inherited a cyberinfrastructure of systems, data, and services that arose from and is optimized for research in science and engineering. As a result, humanists have access to technology but are in search of questions: What scholarship becomes possible when, from their desktops, scholars can access vast stores of admittedly highly heterogeneous data together with powerful capabilities for analysis and presentation? In the terms set by this scene, how do we use comput-

---

[1] The film is based on a novel of the same name by Milan Kundera. The novel was written in 1982 and published in Paris in 1984.

ers as adroitly as the director used the camera to enable research that takes advantage of the capabilities of the technology to tell "the story"—to conduct research and convey findings—in new and important ways? To get beyond, as one participant in a September 15, 2008, symposium on promoting digital scholarship sponsored by CLIR and the National Endowment for the Humanities (NEH) said, treating the computer like "a black box"?

Cyberinfrastructure and Scholarship

We find ourselves at a tipping point. Several decades of research that combines humanities scholarship with computational resources are accumulating into a transition from a field characterized by a series of interesting projects to one that is more cohesive, collaborative, and less confined to the interests of a relatively small number of scholars. Organization of NEH's Office of Digital Humanities signals coalescence of support behind applications of information technology to topics in the humanities. The American Council of Learned Societies' 2007 report, *Our Cultural Commonwealth,* reflected a broad interest in the cyberinfrastructure of research and articulated a sense that the nature of computationally intensive research transcends traditional boundaries. And increased awareness of the value of collaboration is evidenced by the organization of centerNet, Project Bamboo, and a workshop jointly sponsored by the National Science Foundation (NSF), the Institute of Museum and Library Services (IMLS), and NEH in October 2008 on Tools for Data-Driven Scholarship. The National Digital Information Infrastructure and Preservation Program (NDIIPP) at the Library of Congress, its network of partners, and mass digitization projects together with the proliferation of more traditional text conversion and markup projects have created collections of information in digital form in a quantity, diversity, and scale hitherto unknown as well as a community of scholars, librarians, and archivists with a common interest in long-term preservation of digital content. Finally, a generation of young scholars who are comfortable with computational techniques has begun to change the intellectual complexion of traditional faculties, although access to facilities and resources are still unevenly distributed.

These young scholars can feel ghettoized and even disadvantaged when seeking grants and when promotion and tenure review committees evaluate their computationally intensive work.[2] Indeed, many digital humanities centers studied by Diane Zorich in her report for the Scholarly Communication Institute in July 2008, which is summarized in this anthology, were founded in part to provide a sense of community for these scholars. Somewhat paradoxically, these centers now risk becoming silos and may constitute barriers

[2] One participant in the September 15, 2008, meeting argued against the distinction between "humanities" and "digital humanities," noting "Aren't all scholars digital in some ways, even if they simply use the Internet to search?" We agree that this is an important point but have retained the phrase, "digital humanities," since it is now commonly used to identify a specific kind of scholarship.

to the evolving trans-institutional cyberinfrastructure, collaboration, and resource management necessary to achieve efficient allocation of expensive resources and to enable research at a scale that takes into account the wealth of heterogeneous digital source material as well as computational and analytical power.

Zorich's report is part of an extended, distributed conversation that CLIR has sustained over the last 18 months. This conversation ranged broadly over the confluence of cyberinfrastructure, scholarship, and collections, in particular the preservation of those digital collections to enable access, verification of results, and reuse and repurposing of materials. CLIR sponsored two major events, in addition to its contribution to the annual Scholarly Communication Institute. The first was a one-day workshop in November 2007, Promoting Digital Scholarship: Building the Environment, which resulted in a report, *Many More than a Million: Building the Digital Environment for the Age of Abundance* (Crane and Friedlander 2008). The second, mentioned earlier, was the CLIR-NEH symposium, Promoting Digital Scholarship: Formulating Research Challenges in the Humanities, Social Sciences, and Computation, held September 15, 2008. The administrative report, which includes an account of the day's discussion, has been posted to the symposium Web site, where the prospectus, agenda, and list of participants and their brief biographies are also located.[3]

Discussions at the November 2007 symposium had focused on issues that arise as a result of mass digitization projects. Among the recommendations was a call for the articulation of "marquee" research questions, analogous to the grand challenge questions in the sciences, which provide large-scale intellectual coherence without constraining individual or unique projects. This call led directly to the September 2008 symposium, which invited about 30 scholars across the humanities, social sciences, and computer science to look squarely at the role of research questions in promoting new scholarship. The white papers commissioned to frame the discussions appear in this volume and, together with themes in the discussions themselves, form most of the content of the research program described in the remainder of this chapter.

There exists an important but often-ignored distinction between the research programs that rely on an infrastructure and the research infrastructure itself. The term "cyberinfrastructure" originated in a report by the NSF, where it is defined as the comprehensive infrastructure required to capitalize on advances in information technology, which "integrates hardware for computing, data and networks, digitally-enabled sensors, observatories and experimental facilities, and an interoperable suite of software and middleware services and tools" (NSF 2007, 6). The ACLS subsequently adopted the term in *Our Cultural Commonwealth*, and the word has crept into routine discourse in higher education and advanced research. While there is an intimate connection between the instrumentation, software tools and

---

3 See http://www.clir.org/activities/digitalscholar2/.

platforms, resources and facilities, on the one hand, and the research programs on the other, they are, nonetheless, distinct. Yes, research is conducted on the infrastructure—how to make it better, faster, more reliable, and, in a sense, smarter. But that work is distinct from the research that the infrastructure has been invented and optimized to enable and support. So if the infrastructure answers the question, *how*?, the research program answers the questions *what?* and *why?*

Undoubtedly tools are important. They are common features of digital humanities centers, can do many things researchers want to do, and are concrete. They can be evaluated and compared according to agreed-upon protocols, like the "evaluation-guided research paradigm" that Douglas Oard describes in his essay, which consists of the challenge problem (perhaps a set of texts to be classified), the answer key (the correct answers), and the evaluation measure (the fraction of the system's assignments that are considered "right").[4] Humanists have developed a plethora of tools of varying quality, few of them apparently used by more than a relative handful of scholars.[5] In response, one of the symposium participants recommended that digital humanists generally had to become more disciplined about evaluating the utility of their tools. Indeed, Project Bamboo and the October 2008 Tools for Data Driven Scholarship workshop are steps in precisely that direction.

But tools can also deflect attention. "Are we letting our anxieties about tools and protocols and methodologies obscure bigger questions?" a scholar of medieval literature asked in the CLIR-NEH September 2008 symposium, before observing that methods, protocols, and disciplines gradually evolve only after the need for a function or capability has been perceived. Historically, research has driven the development of cyberinfrastructure, whose roots trace back to the development of computer networking in the 1960s and advances in high performance computing in the 1980s. These technologies enabled organization of distributed research teams and access to data and other resources as well as computationally intensive analysis in a range of fields in the life sciences, social sciences, and physical sciences. After listening to some of the discussion, one of the computer scientists at the September 2008 symposium suggested that humanities scholars need to "get to the next level of problem definition, perhaps talking about the tasks they need solved (such as finding something particular in text) rather than the system they need built." This comment resonated with a recommendation from another computer scientist, a specialist in human-computer interfaces and design, who advised humanists to be able to answer the question, "What is it you

---

[4] It is used for example in the well-known TREC competitions, run annually by the National Institute of Standards and Technology (NIST), which seek to support research within the information retrieval community by enabling large-scale evaluation of text retrieval methodologies; see Text REtrieval Conference, http://trec.nist.gov/.

[5] Humanities' tools have not been systematically studied; this occasioned the workshop on Tools for Data-Driven Scholarship in October 2008. One example of evaluation of two aspects of tools—their findability and usability—is Nguyen and Shilton 2008. CLIR has commissioned a follow-up study on tools and infrastructure, which is scheduled for release in the summer of 2009.

are trying to do?" and to explain the kinds of evidence that would be necessary to adduce to answer a given question rather than focusing on the available technologies or the technologies they believe are available. Embedded in these remarks are different notions of what constitutes a question. Indeed, questions exist at many scales, and famous scientific grand challenge questions (for example, the relationship between electricity and magnetism) in practice resolved into a series of questions that converged on an answer over the centuries.

Humanists do not lack for questions. For example, Gregory Crane wants to understand how the contemporary Islamic Republic of Iran arose from the Persian Empire of antiquity, a question that requires an enormous array of disparate sources in many languages spanning centuries. Anthropologists and archaeologists want to delineate the prehistoric migrations to the Americas. Medieval scholars want to plumb the surviving manuscripts and compare them in ways not possible in analog and thus reinterpret the texts themselves. In so doing, Stephen Nichols has argued, the modern reader confronts the original texts the way the original readers did—without the intermediary of the nineteenth century standard editions (Nichols 2008).

Posing questions at the right level of abstraction, as suggested by one of the participants, is non-trivial. Answering "big" or "marquee" questions that provide high-level coherence and allow individual scholars to find common ground with others engaged in related research requires experimentation as well as consensus building. The next step of parsing these marquee questions into operational questions is its own intellectual exercise that may involve exploration to see what exists or happens when a technique is tried before a formal research project is posed. Moreover, the term *humanities* is misleading in the sense that it imparts high-level unity where in fact, humanities scholarship subsumes an array of disciplines from archaeology and art history to literary criticism to history of science, each with its own literatures, methods, and traditions. Yet there is a sense that there is sufficient common ground to articulate a shared infrastructure of tools, services, and collections that would reduce unnecessary redundancy, allocate human and information resources efficiently, and, most interestingly, enable a different kind of scholarship.

Caroline Levander makes the latter point when she argues that the deep significance of Our Americas Archive Project (OAAP) is its ability to restructure the categories of knowledge precisely by restructuring collections related to the Americas and hence access to materials, so that the structure of the collections helps scholars "pry [their research] loose" from the self-limiting assumptions of the nation state. Some at the symposium suggested that boundaries be cast differently, perhaps, for example, to see the Atlantic world as a historically coherent framework of population and economic interchange rather than defining the scope as continental landmasses. Nevertheless, no one quarreled with her fundamental insight: that the organization of collections is inherent in the way that research is framed, that such organization of knowledge bounds the way that research is then undertaken, and that challenges to conceptual boundaries can sometimes begin with the organization of source material.

Questions and Collaborations

If this new scholarship is to be more than a series of boutique projects that use computers, one component must be a set of organizational topics and questions that do not bind research into legacy categories and do invite interesting collaborations that will allow for creative cross-fertilization of ideas and techniques and then spur new questions to be pursued by colleagues and students. Collaboration across traditional boundaries is particularly important for ambitious projects that require years of research and cannot be summed up in a single dissertation or monograph. However, collaboration is a social as well as an intellectual process and can be difficult for many reasons, some of them having to do with institutional and disciplinary cultures, language and terminology, mental models about the research process, trust, appropriate credit, and a sensible allocation of tasks.[6] For example, Andreas Paepcke points to the "agenda mismatch" between the requirements of the domain scholar and the trajectory of computer science research, typically done by a doctoral student. The student's product is usually a prototype; it works "well enough." "Well enough" is probably not sufficient for most humanities scholars, but the time required to create the robust tool is not justified in terms of the student's career path (Paepcke 2008).[7] So one metric that this computer science researcher uses to determine a suitable collaborative project is the project's ability to yield publishable research in peer-reviewed journals for *both* lead investigators.

The key is the appropriate level of abstraction, that is to say, questions and topics that represent major areas of research, are broad enough to embrace a number of related topics, and allow individual researchers to find an intellectual home. They are not so narrow as to constrain the research nor so expansive as to be meaningless. In the discussions that have taken place, we have observed four themes that transcend traditional disciplinary boundaries and resonate with major research topics in computer science: scale, language and communication, space and time, and social networking. The boundaries between them are indistinct, and techniques that are developed in one may apply to problems in another.

---

[6] Collaboration in science has been extensively studied. For example, see Hackett 2005. On the specific issues cited here, see Olson et al. n.d.

[7] Others at the September 15 symposium concurred with Paepcke's observations about mismatches in expectations between computer scientists and domain scientists. One researcher said that tools existed that would be of interest to humanists yet using them would be arduous because the interfaces were "abhorrent" and not intuitive to relatively naïve users. She said, "It is not the algorithms but how people can make use of and interact with them that is still so far behind."

Scale

Issues of scale resonate across many disciplines and conversations.[8] The most obvious evidence of scale for humanists is access to heterogeneous digital information of varying quality and in quantities that were unimaginable in prior generations, creating what Crane has dubbed "the million book problem." That is, "even if we could marshal the resources to do so, the human life contains only about 30,000 days—reading a book a day we would only finish a million books after thirty lifetimes of reading. Only machines can process or 'read,' much less analyze, the written record of humanity." So analyzing material at scale requires computation. Scale also means diversity. Collections will increasingly include images, video, and audio, as well as multiple languages, many of them using different scripts requiring transliteration and cross-language capabilities. Some of this information will have been formally ingested into well-managed archives; some will be captured on the fly and deposited into repositories with minimal attention. Making sense of this welter of material implies authenticating the sources through new, automated methods and combining them in creative ways to answer important questions and employing increasingly powerful machines and creative strategies[9] to do so.

Computationally intensive research allows for both very expansive and very detailed investigations. For example, nineteenth-century railroading in the United States has been extensively studied in part because the history can be read as a proxy for the importance of technology and transportation in promoting economic growth, both core questions in economics with clear implications for public policies. Scale allows for both international and subregional comparisons, as Will Thomas, an historian at the University of Nebraska, has suggested (Crane and Friedlander 2008). Scale also allows for greater detail. Dan Cohen, an historian at George Mason University and director of the Center of Technology and the New Media, has pointed out that tracking references to the Bible and/or to specific religious terminology across thousands of text references allows rigorous examination of the secularization thesis, which states that the role of religion declined in general discourse during the nineteenth century. Other topics might include analysis of the poetry cited in popular literature such as magazines and newspapers, or the changing role of Shakespeare as seen by the plays mentioned and passages quoted (Crane and Friedlander 2008).

---

[8] Scientists face a "tsunami" of data, one participant said, and in 2007, the volume of information created is estimated to have exceeded available storage capacity (see Gantz et al. 2008). Not all of that data should be archived. Nevertheless, current capacity to store, manage, access, retrieve, and repurpose information is reaching its limits. Even IT professionals who focus directly on storage systems acknowledge, "The data center process and archive system is technologically broken. It doesn't scale" (Peterson et al. 2007, 7-8).

[9] For a concise discussion of some of the technologies required to create, store, manage, and analyze large data sets, see Purdue University 2003.

Language and Communication

Developing evidence to the questions posed by Thomas and Cohen relies on linguistic and geospatial techniques, the second and third themes. Language is central to much of humanities scholarship, and many of the early digital humanities projects revolved around markup of text converted from analog to ASCII.[10] In addition to the traditional projects that typically combine scanned images with marked-up text, the mass digitization projects are yielding extremely large digital corpora that are both problematic from the perspective of quality (Duguid 2007) and fascinating from the perspective of their content. As Oard explains, human language actually exists in several forms: spoken, written, and character-encoded—that is, the digital representation of language—as well as sign. His paper provides a context for understanding some of the research computer scientists and linguists conduct. It is complemented by the paper by Crane and his colleagues, who examine the role of several of these techniques in the context of classics and philology with the twin goals of increasing scholars' access to more materials while expanding the potential audiences for their work.

The research potential is obvious in several dimensions. The scale, complexity, and heterogeneity of the material challenge researchers to make sense of the data, to find patterns at multiple levels (book, page, paragraph, sentence), detect anomalies, and derive meaning. Such corpora represent a rich source for cross-language studies[11] and create an opportunity for language and text-intensive disciplines in the humanities to become partners in the research process, as Oard argues, because their research materials can also offer challenging problem sets that are central to the way language systems are built and evaluated. Advances in capture technologies and broadened participation in the research process imply that different kinds of content, notably speech, can be taken into multiformat research collections and made discoverable through unified search not only to ethnographers and linguists but also to literary scholars, art historians, archaeologists, and students and researchers who might not otherwise think of these kinds of sources as relevant to their studies.[12]

---

10 For example, see the rich set of articles in Siemens and Schreibman 2008.

11 Note that China, Japan, and South Korea combined now account for 27 percent of world research and development (R&D), and China is second in the number of scientists and engineers engaged in research activities. Substantial contributions to the global scientific literature may not be published in English. In this context, machine translation systems as well as other forms of document analysis, recognition, summarization, and categorization take on practical urgency; see http://www.aaas.org/spp/rd/guiintl.htm. According to the analysis by the American Association for the Advancement of Science based on data from the Organization for Economic Cooperation and Development in 2007, the United States still led the world in its investment in R&D with 36 percent of projected world R&D performance.

12 The Oyez project is a multimedia archive, combining audio, images, and text, devoted to the Supreme Court of the United States and its work has demonstrated the potential of such integration of sources. It is both a source for all audio recorded in the Court since the installation of a recording system in October 1955 and has been a testbed for experiments in audio capture. See http://www.oyez.org/about/.

Searching[13] across large, heterogeneous collections is obviously important. But the technologies create other opportunities for analysis and presentation. For example, visualization is one way that investigators can identify patterns and detect anomalies in large corpora as well as display results. Moreover, there is substantial evidence that the next generation will be graphical learners and communicators (Fisch 2007), implying that visualization will become increasingly important as a means of analysis as well as a mode of presentation and communication. Maureen Stone explores the topic of visualization, emphasizing the need to educate consumers as well as users of graphical media. The Web, which is an inherently graphical and interactive medium, increases the likelihood of confusion and misinformation; it requires an expanded notion of literacy, she argues. She cites a number of examples in which an image was either based on inaccurate information or was constructed in a way that conveyed confusing or inaccurate information, offering the hypothetical example of pricing information over time that fails to control for inflation (or price indexing).

There is some historical precedent for such concerns. During the 1884 presidential elections in the United States, a map of the western states and territories was published in which the proposed route of the transcontinental railroads through public lands was indicated by a thick black line. It occasioned an outcry over an apparent land grab by the railroad barons. In fact, the line had been drawn without regard for scale or for the rather convoluted terms of the grants, which had made shares in the companies that held these grants all but impossible to sell (Henry 1966).

Space and Time

Maps are a form of visualization, and visualization is closely linked to geographical information systems (GIS) and simulations. Both are intrinsic to the third theme, time and space. Geographers, one of the participants observed, have made considerable headway with space but time is still a problem. Space and time have been manifested in different ways in humanities scholarship. One obvious way is the organization of a collection of materials, reference tools, and analytical services by geography and period, like the OAAP or the Persepolis Fortification Archive Project. Space and time may encompass the detailed work of establishing provenance, authenticity, and versioning of source material, which becomes difficult and therefore interesting in the messy and heterogeneous output of mass digitization projects. Or, scholars may seek to understand the use of terms and phrases over time, as Cohen has suggested. Jonathan Bengston outlined work at the John M. Kelly Library at the St. Michael's College in the University of Toronto to coordinate an effort to digitize the works of John Henry Newman, feed the digitized output into a

13 We are aware that the term "searching" in this context is actually a shorthand that embodies a larger array of behaviors (e.g., browsing and discovery) and technologies, including information retrieval, human computer interface design, database and repository systems.

document analysis system, and identify subtle changes in language and meaning. Longer term, he speculates, it will be even more interesting to see if relationships can be traced between the evolution of Newman's thought and the wider intellectual milieu by comparing this database of materials with larger corpora at a far more granular level than has been achieved by traditional scholarly methods (Crane and Friedlander 2008).

The notion of "space" can mean also physical or social spaces and their historical changes, where visualization and simulation can be very powerful. Archaeologists have taken advantage of the digital medium to render their information in three-dimensional modes, allowing virtual reconstructions of their sites that provide views that cannot be obtained even on the physical site itself.[14] Stephen Murray, an historian of French gothic cathedrals, uses a mix of capture and display technologies to re-create or simulate the three-dimensional spaces so that his students can also re-experience the soaring interiors at an otherwise inaccessible level of detail and to demonstrate relationships among resources that are geographically separate. He argues that this pedagogical technique removes the cathedral from its status as a fully formed and static object represented by a slide in a darkened lecture hall and allows students to understand that these were works in progress over a period of decades, embodying countless choices and decisions. For the symposium, he demonstrated a simulation that employed engineering algorithms to simulate the stresses on a Romanesque arch as it was made larger to show that the transition from the rounded Romanesque form to the pointed Gothic form was an aesthetic and a structural choice.

As these examples demonstrate, phenomena have been reinterpreted over different times and at different scales, and materials associated with an individual, group of individuals, theme, or with geographical spaces have been assembled to create collections characterized by richly marked-up text, concordances, and other reference tools. Scale, as Bengston's example demonstrates, allows this kind of focused work to become expanded. Scale also allows for conceptualizing more complex projects incorporating other types of data—in particular, scientific datasets that might allow for reconstructions and simulations of early landscapes, climate, and habitat. As one participant commented, interesting work is possible in simulating development of cities or agrarian societies, providing opportunities for multidisciplinary synthesis that is difficult to achieve without involving data on geography, weather, construction, social history, and so on. Certainly the demographic data assembled by the Minnesota Population Center or curated by the Inter-university Consortium for Political and Social Research are obvious candidates for such integrative research, as are the environmental collections

[14] A simple search of the Web using the terms "archaeology" and "simulation" yielded 554,000 hits. The 20 most highly ranked covered (1) journal articles that used simulation techniques to do site reconstructions and artifact distributions, (2) references to a textbook on use of simulation in archaeology that is in press, (3) conferences and seminars, and (4) use of site simulation software to teach archaeological methods.

managed by the University Corporation for Atmospheric Research and others. At the same time, the potential of historic travelers and explorers' accounts to add temporal depth to ecological and environmental studies is substantial but difficult to use.

Extracting the relevant information from texts, manuscripts, and drawings is a challenging technical problem, as Oard's essay suggests. Still, the nineteenth and early twentieth-century collections of specimens together with the field notes and laboratory descriptions represent a potential wealth of biological information that could enable reconstructions of historic landscapes that might inform research in literature and art history as well as ecology, environmental studies, and climate studies.[15] Layering such information onto the already complex problem of normalizing heterogeneous sources in the social sciences (Berman and Brady 2005) increases the complexity. But it remains a topic where analysis of text, language, history, and science may intersect and where GIS, visualization, simulation, and linguistic and statistical tools all have roles.

Social Networking

Bengston's example of questions that might be posed of Newman's papers calls attention to the relationships in the information as well as to discerning patterns in the use of language. Social networking, described by Bernardo Huberman, is simultaneously a technique (or set of techniques) and an object of study. This paper excited substantial discussion during the symposium, and in it he argues that the web of information represents a network of social relationships as well as a technological network. The information can be read to expose relationships that might not be otherwise evident and to illustrate how the specific technologies affect the allocation of human attention. There have been similar findings, as Huberman acknowledges, and the significance of this work lies in its scale, rigor, and level of abstraction; the algorithms can be applied in any body of work where the links can be established.

Social network analysis, one participant noted, has been successfully used in national security analyses.[16] Like GIS or visualization, these social networking algorithms represent a set of analytics that could be used to characterize text corpora, enabling researchers to identify patterns and detect anomalies more generally. For example, the scholar of Old Norse suggested that these analytics could be used to "map the social network in [Icelandic] sagas over time and then

---

15 As a step in this direction, CLIR recently funded the cataloging of botanical collections at University and Jepson Herbaria, University of California, Berkeley, as part of the Hidden Collections program. For more information on this program, see http://www.clir.org/hiddencollections/index.html.

16 The Visualizing Patterns in Databases of Cultural Images and Video project proposes to identify such patterns in heterogeneous data. Led by Lev Manovich, director of the Software Studies Initiative at the University of California, San Diego, the project was among those recently funded under the NEH High Performance Computing Program; see Cultural Analytics, http://lab.softwarestudies.com/2008/09/cultural-analytics.html, and Humanities and High Performance Computers Connect at NERSC, December 22, 2008; http://newscenter.lbl.gov/feature-stories/2008/12/22/humanitiesnersc/.

perhaps integrate with GIS and use this to try to draw actual historic and geographic interpretations." Equally importantly, Huberman's essay calls attention to the importance of studying the Web as an object. It ceases to be a neutral technology but instead affects the outcomes by amplifying and instantiating certain behaviors. In short, the Web is the new "text" for humanities scholarship.

What Comes Next?

Infrastructure is both social and engineered and is built from both the bottom up and the top down. It has historically been successful when local needs align with regional and national goals and when local activities take place within a sometimes loosely organized, yet coherent framework. The current landscape in digital scholarship is replete with examples of bottom-up enterprise; the open question is whether and how to stimulate large-scale coherence without stymieing individual enterprise, frustrating existing self-organization, or threatening the individualism that traditionally characterizes humanities research. The infrastructure itself is so costly and the potential gains from collaborative research are so appealing that some form of loose coordination seems appropriate.

We believe that research should drive the large-scale coherence to enable scholars of diverse backgrounds and interests to devise rich new projects and work creatively across disciplines, including computer science, while avoiding the continued proliferation of stovepipes. One participant observed, "We need to think holistically about the integration of all of these services and tools in terms of the user experience—we don't want to create multiple fragmented environments." Many participants called for various kinds of demonstration projects that would, as one scholar noted, show "people that computational tools will help them." Such projects, she continued, let "people explore new methodologies" and see how results can be transferred from one project to another. The four themes or topics that have been proposed as an initial umbrella—scale, language and communication, space and time, and social networking—tap into well-established communities of researchers. Projects conceived in this framework are likely to be robust enough to accommodate both team-based and single-investigator approaches as well as avoid the pitfall Paepcke has called "agenda mismatch," where the results of the collaboration are sufficient for the computer science student but sadly wanting for the humanities researcher.

In addition to agreeing on the importance of research as a long-term driver and the importance of demonstration projects, symposium participants offered some concrete next steps. Several proposed formulating ontologies as one avenue for future collaborative research. The term "ontologies" as used by computer and information scientists can be confusing to some humanities scholars who may have first encountered the word in an introductory course on the history of philosophy where it meant studying the nature of reality. A computational ontology is a hierarchical organization of a domain of knowledge that a machine can process with the most general categories at the top and the most specific categories at the bottom. In a forthcoming article for the journal *Synthese* (anticipated late 2009), Cameron Buckner, Mathias Niepert, and Colin Allen offer the example, "*Wine* ➔ *Red Wine* ➔ *Beaujolais;*" everything that "is a" instance of *Beaujolas* "is a" instance of *Red Wine*, and everything that "is a" instance of *Red Wine* "is a" instance of *Wine.*"[17] Although some work has been done, no large teams have formed, despite the fact that there is substantial interdisciplinary potential in such collaborations between domain specialists and computer scientists. Ontologies can be used to capture the formalization of basic concepts and can then inform more sophisticated tools and systems that are directly relevant to coping with both scale and language.

Another practical recommendation, echoed by several participants, was to create test sets that can afford investigators opportunities to experiment and learn. The most ambitious version of this idea consisted of putting existing large text corpora on powerful computer systems where researchers could explore some of the possibilities. On the basis of that experimentation, innovative questions that several people called for might emerge, thus addressing the intellectual problems inherent in asking the "right questions." At the same time, the shared resource becomes central to the structure of a discipline or set of disciplines whose research depends on it. One participant asked rhetorically, "What is the Protein Data Bank for the humanities?" And by extension, where is the motivation to support long-term preservation of these resources?

One answer to her question is: all the libraries, archives, museums, and collections of the world. So in a sense, there is no analogy, digital or otherwise, in humanities scholarship to the role of some of the key scientific datasets. But there are shared, enduring values and protocols about methods and evidence, about what constitutes an acceptable argument, and about the importance of the integrity of the source material and the research on which it is based, thus putting primacy on the importance of continuing to build sustainable and reliable collections. The challenges associated with technology-intensive management of digital collections over time are substantial, but the goals of these collections are clear: They must allow digital collections to be explored, expanded, and repurposed as the research questions evolve, and users must trust the data repositories both to safeguard their contents and to serve up reliable and trustworthy data sets upon request. Building and managing digital collections remains a fundamental condition for any research agenda.

---

[17] Colin Allen, personal communication by e-mail, January 16, 2009. Professor Allen graciously explained the concept of ontologies and provided additional background from the cited forthcoming article in the journal *Synthese*, anticipated late 2009. A version of the article, jointly authored by Buckner, Niepert, and Allen, can be found at http://inpho.cogs.indiana.edu/Papers/TaxonomizingIdeas.pdf.

References

American Council of Learned Societies Commission on Cyberinfrastructure for the Humanities and Social Sciences. 2007. *Our Cultural Commonwealth*. New York: ACLS.

Berman, Francine, and Henry Brady. May 12, 2005. *Final Report: NSF SBE-CISE Workshop on Cyberinfrastructure and the Social Science,* p. 9, 18-21. Available at www.sdsc.edu/sbe/.

Crane, Gregory, and Amy Friedlander. 2008. Many More than a Million: Building the Digital Environment for the Age of Abundance. Report of a One-day Seminar on Promoting Digital Scholarship, November 28, 2007. Council on Library and Information Resources. Available at http://www.clir.org/activities/digitalscholar/Nov28final.pdf.

Duguid, Paul. 2007. Inheritance and Loss? A Brief Survey of Google Books. *First Monday* 12(8). Available at http://firstmonday.org/issues/issue12_8/duguid/index.html.

Fisch, Karl. 2007. The Fischbowl: Did you know? Shift happens, 2.0, June 22, 2007. Available at http://thefischbowl.blogspot.com/2007/06/did-you-know-20.html

Gantz, John F., Chrisopher Chute, Alex Manfrediz, Stephen Minton, David Reinsel, Wolfgang Schlichting, and Anna Toncheva. March 2008. The Diverse and Exploding Digital Universe: An Update Forecast of Worldwide Information Growth Through 2011, pp. 2, 3. Framingham, Mass.: IDC.

Hackett, Edward J., ed. 2005. Special Issue: Scientific Collaboration, *Social Studies of Science* 35(5).

Henry, Robert S. 1966. The Railroad Land Grant Legend in American History Texts. In Carl N. Degler, ed., *Pivotal Interpretations of American History*, Vol. II, pp. 36-66. New York: Harper & Row Publishers.

National Science Foundation Cyberinfrastructure Council. March 2007. *Cyberinfrastructure Vision for 21st Century Discovery*, 6.

Nguyen, Lilly, and Katie Shilton. 2008. Tools for Humanists. Appendix F in Diane M. Zorich, *A Survey of Digital Humanities Centers in the United States*. Washington, DC: Council on Library and Information Resources, 58-78. Available at http://www.clir.org/pubs/abstract/pub143abst.html.

Nichols, Stephen G. 2008. "Born Medieval": MSS. in the Digital Scriptorium. *Journal of Electronic Publishing* 11(1). Available at http://dx.doi.org/10.3998/3336451.0011.104.

Olson, Judith S., Garry M. Olson, and Erik C. Hofer. n.d. What makes for success in science and engineering collaboratories. Available at http://www-unix.mcs.anl.gov/fl/flevents/wace/wace2005/talks/olson-wace2005.pdf.

Paepcke, Andreas. 2008. An Often Ignored Collaboration Pitfall: Time Phase Agenda Mismatch. Blog posting to Stanford iLab November 8.

Peterson, Michael, Gary Zasman, Peter Mojica, Jeff Porter. 2007. 100 Year Archive Requirements Survey, pp. 7-8. Storage Network Industry Association. Available at http://www.snia.org/forums/dmf/programs/ltacsi/forums/dmf/programs/ltacsi/100_year/100YrATF_Archive-Requirements-Survey_20070619.pdf.

Purdue University. 2003. Massive Data: Management, Analysis, Visualization, and Security: A School of Science Focus Area, May 15, 2003. Available at http://www.science.purdue.edu/about_us/strategic_plan/COALESCEAreas/MassiveData03may.pdf. This is a chapter in the 2003-2008 Strategic Plan (http://www.science.purdue.edu/about_us/strategic_plan/) developed by the College of Science, Purdue University.

Siemens, Ray, and Susan Schreibman, eds. 2008. *A Companion to Digital Literary Studies*. Oxford: Blackwell. Available at http://www.digitalhumanities.org/companionDLS/.

Web sites

centerNet: An International Network of Digital Humanities Center; http://www.digitalhumanities.org/centernet/.

The Minnesota Population Center, 2003-2008; http://www.pop.umn.edu/.

National Digital Information Infrastructure Preservation Program. Digital Preservation, Library of Congress; http://www.digitalpreservation.gov.

Persepolis Fortification Archive; http://oi.uchicago.edu/research/projects/pfa/.

Project Bamboo; http://projectbamboo.uchicago.edu/.

Tools for Data-Driven Scholarship; http://mith.umd.edu/tools/.

University Corporation for Atmospheric Research—UCAR & NCAR; http://www.ucar.edu/.

Tools for Thinking: ePhilology and Cyberinfrastructure

Gregory Crane, Alison Babeu, David Bamman, Lisa Cerrato, Rashmi Singhal

Philology brings back to life the words of languages no longer spoken. While literally "the love of language," philology includes not only linguistics but philosophy, history, literary criticism, the history of science and technology, political science, economics, art, archaeology, and every other discipline relevant to the world that these texts describe. Of course, philology must, in its fullest form, engage fully with the material record: museum collections and archeological excavations not only serve to illustrate topics within the text but also provide independent windows onto the past from which we may survey views very different from those we glimpse in the texts alone. Philology is thus not just about text; it is about the world that produced our surviving textual sources and about the tangible impact that these texts have had upon the worlds that read them.[1]

Few of us manage to be philologists in this broad sense. We cannot, with the tools of print technology, cover enough intellectual ground. Even if we set aside, for the moment, the problem of working with material culture, and consider only the challenges of textual materials easily represented in print form, our limitations are severe. As Solon points out in *The History of Herodotus*, there are only about 30,000 days in a human life—at a book a day, we would need 30 generations to read through even a moderate collection of a million books and 10,000 years to cover the 10 million-or-so unique items in the Harvard Library system.

The barriers are not simply quantitative. Few of us will ever be able to finish a cursory reading of 10 books, however thin, if these

1 For some further exploration of the new challenges of e-philology, see G. Crane, D. Bamman, and A. Babeu. 2008. ePhilology: When the Books Talk to Their Readers. In *A Companion to Digital Literary Studies*, edited by Ray Siemens and Susan Schreibman. New York: Blackwell Publishing, 29–64.

books contain untranslated poems in 10 different languages. Classical philologists must have expertise in Greek and Latin and an ability to work with scholarship in English, French, German, and Italian. If, however, we wish to explore broader topics that cut across multiple cultures, e.g., the impact of Genghis Khan and his successors or the rise of Christianity and Islam, then we soon confront sources in far more languages than most scholars can expect to master. And indeed, in many cases mastery may not be an issue: scholars are still rapidly expanding our ability to understand languages such as Sumerian and Mayan. In cases such as classical Greek, Sanskrit, and Chinese, by contrast, so much information survives that we must remain students for our entire lives.

The great challenge for the rising generation of scholars is to build a digital infrastructure with which to expand our intellectual range.[2] We seek to advance two effects already enabled by the digital infrastructure at hand. On the one hand, we are extending the intellectual range of individual scholars, enabling them to pursue topics that require analysis of more primary sources or more linguistic materials than was feasible with print. Mark Schiefsky's work with Archimedes illustrates how scholars were able to explore a broad historical topic (in this case, the history of mechanics) with greater rigor than would have been possible in print—assuming they would have undertaken such an ambitious project at all. At the same time, we want to increase the complementary effect and further extend the audiences that the products of particular cultures can reach. Machine translation is one technology that aims to advance this goal, but even the simple translation-support systems already provided in environments such as the Perseus Digital Library have for years made foreign language texts intellectually more accessible to students than print resources alone.

We can already see new classes of research project taking shape. Thus, we could, with existing technology, build collections and services in which we could study the influence of Plato across a wide range of cultures, including not only every written language from the history of Europe but Arabic and Persian as well. Multilingual named entity identification systems would scan these corpora for references to Plato, for translations of his works, and for quotations of particular passages.[3] Text-mining systems would summarize pat-

---

[2] A good overview of the challenges of building a digital infrastructure in the humanities, as well as a survey of much of the recent literature on the topic, can be found in D. Green and M. Roy. 2008. Things to Do While Waiting for the Future to Happen: Building a Cyberinfrastructure for the Liberal Arts. *EDUCAUSE Review* 43(4), available at http://connect.educause.edu/display/46969. For a look at some of the specific challenges for building a cyberinfrastructure in classics, see D. Pritchard. 2008. Working Papers, Open Access, and Cyber-infrastructure in Classical Studies. *Literary and Linguistic Computing* 23(2): 149–162.

[3] Multilingual systems for named entity recognition is an area of research that is growing rapidly. For some interesting recent work in this area, see C. Silberer, et al. 2008. Building a Multilingual Lexical Resource for Named Entity Disambiguation, Translation and Transliteration. *Proceedings of the Sixth International Language Resources and Evaluation (LREC'08)*, 3230-3237. Available at http://www.lrec-conf.org/proceedings/lrec2008/pdf/816_paper.pdf.

terns of thought associated with Plato and his works.[4] Word- and phrase-translation systems would allow us to extract the meanings of these key phrases in languages with which we are not familiar. We could even begin to align patterns in different languages, perhaps revealing that discourse about Plato in ninth-century Arabic is more closely related to that in Persian than to that in nineteenth-century German—or perhaps not.

These automated processes are only a starting point. Like the infrastructure of modern athletic training, our intellectual infrastructure only allows us to use our limited cognitive resources to greater effect. Our customization and personalization systems would use models of our educational background and immediate purposes[5] to provide us with the briefing materials necessary to begin evaluating what we see: pointers to translations into languages with which we are familiar (e.g., from Persian into French), automatically generated lists of new words and concepts in sources where we have studied the documents, pre-existing encyclopedia entries, and automatically generated key phrases in recent scholarship about people, places, organizations and readily identified topics (e.g., Plato's *Republic*).

We already have the algorithms, and Google—or the Google partner libraries with noncommercial rights to books digitized from their collections—have the collections[6] that would open new areas of research that become possible only when we can automatically analyze collections far too big and far too heterogeneous for any human brain.

Consider one concrete example. In 2010, 2,500 years will have passed since the Greeks confronted an army from the Persian Empire on the plains of Marathon. After 10 years of training, a junior classicist might have extensive, but hardly exhaustive, knowledge of the scholarship surrounding Herodotus's accounts of the Persian Wars in the early fifth century or the major Greek sources about Alexander's invasion of Persia a century and a half later. With a good deal of effort, the junior classicist could develop an undergraduate survey course about Greek and Persian relations, as seen from Greek and Latin sources. One scholar suggested in private correspondence that 95 percent of the research on Alexander the Great involves scholars

---

[4] The potential of text mining for humanities texts has been explored in recent years by various researchers. For some recent work, see A. Don, et al. 2007. Discovering Interesting Usage Patterns in Text Collections: Integrating Text Mining With Visualization. *Proceedings of the Sixteenth ACM Conference on Information Knowledge Management*, 213–222.

[5] Customization and personalization systems that utilize user models to adapt information to the reader's needs have been explored by many researchers, such as F. Ahmad, et al. 2007. Towards Automatic Conceptual Personalization Tools. *JCDL 2007: Proceedings of the 7th ACM/IEEE CS-Joint Conference on Digital Libraries*, 452-461; and E. Frias Martinez, et al. 2006. Automated User Modeling For Personalized Digital Libraries. *International Journal of Information Management* 26(3): 234–248.

[6] An article by Grogg and Ashmore explores how Google partner libraries vary in what they are doing with their digital copies. See J. E. Grogg and B. Ashmore. 2007. Google Book Search Libraries and their Digital Copies. *Searcher* 15(4). Available at http://www.infotoday.com/searcher/apr07/Grogg_Ashmore.shtml.

who do not know a word of Old Persian and have no substantive knowledge of Iranian civilization. Whether or not this admittedly subjective estimate is accurate, the multiethnic and multilingual nature of the Persian Empire has split the subject into small, isolated communities.

There are two problems. First, scholars simply do not have physical access to the sources illustrating Iranian civilization. Second, even if they did have physical access, few can read Farsi, or even put their hands on the background materials needed to contextualize sources about Iranian civilization. Even if the information is available in our existing library collections, scholars are not synthesizing that information. Scholars have adapted their work to the limits of what they can accomplish. All responsible scholars of Alexander would welcome an infrastructure that would allow them to understand the subject as widely as possible. Existing scholarship reflects harsh compromises, as scholars learned what their cognitive resources could accomplish in the tools of print. We need a digital infrastructure that can assemble primary and secondary sources now scattered throughout specialized publications and then provide the background information that each scholar needs to carry on his or her work.

This leads us to the second major advance of the emerging digital infrastructure: if we can change the intellectual range of individual human thinkers, we can also increase the audience for individual products of human culture. By automatically linking inflected words in a text to linguistic analyses and dictionary entries, we have already allowed readers to spend more time thinking about the text than was possible as they flipped through print dictionaries. Reading-support tools allow readers to understand linguistic sources at an earlier stage of their training and to ask questions, no matter how advanced their knowledge, that were not feasible in print.[7] In effect, as we provide more and more sophisticated reading support, we extend the intellectual reach of complex cultural productions.

More than 2,000 years ago, Plato's Socrates questioned the value of written information if it is not converted to active knowledge in a human brain. If we in the humanities had to choose, many of us would agree that it is more important to help the current body of ideas about antiquity play a more vibrant role in human society than to produce new ideas intellectually accessible to their established audiences (i.e., those with years of training and with professional access to libraries that pay for digital subscriptions), but we might find ourselves hard-pressed to make a decision. Some, perhaps most, of us who are professional humanists believe that we have a primary obligation to make the human record play the most dynamic

[7] Reading support tools that help readers more effectively mine their way through digital text is a growing area of research. For some interesting examples, see E. H. Chi, et al. 2007. ScentIndex and ScentHighlights: Productive Reading Techniques for Conceptually Reorganizing Subject Indexes and Highlighting Passages. *Information Visualization* 6(1): 32–47; and C. Faire and N. Vincent. 2007. Document Image Analysis for Active Reading. *Proceedings of the International Workshop on Semantically Aware Document Processing and Indexing,* Montpellier, France, May 21-22, 2007, pp. 7–14.

role possible in the intellectual life of humanity. The two go hand in hand: the more intellectual activity around a topic, the more intellectual labor available. Gutenberg printed Latin bibles. Martin Luther, William Tyndale, and others, building on the technology of print, translated the Bible and fostered intellectual communities that had not previously existed. They changed the world.

It would be easy enough to explore in 2010 the Greco-Roman view of the Battle of Marathon 2,500 years before. We would, however, rather broaden the discussion and engage Iranian scholars to provide their perspectives on the Achaemenid Empire. Ideally, the major sources, including both the textual and material record, would be freely available in digital form, with reading support and other background information in place. Those of us who have dedicated our lives to the study of the Greco-Roman world would welcome the tools whereby we could understand, as deeply as possible, how the fifth-century BCE appears to those who see the Persian Empire as their cultural heritage and be able to study the sources on which that perspective rests.

From Scholar-Centered Publications to Reader-Centered Infrastructure

Perhaps the most important point of continuity—and the greatest reason why publication in classics has adapted so little to the digital world—appears before we even begin reading the publications themselves. An informal survey of 41 e-classics publications available online from Johns Hopkins University Press reveals that 40 (97.5 percent)[8] are products of a single author. The only exception was an archaeological publication in *Hesperia*, the journal of the American School at Athens. While expanding this survey would provide greater statistical certainty, the conclusion would be the same: classicists in 2008 devote most of their energies to individual expressions of particular arguments.

Single-author publications will remain important, but even they can adapt to the digital. Athenian democracy was a major cultural event in human history, and it deserves careful study. So much scholarship has accumulated around this topic that recent professional

[8] This informal survey examined the articles in sample issues that Johns Hopkins made publicly available for marketing purposes. Where there was not a public issue, the most recent online issue was examined. Seven single-author articles in http://muse.jhu.edu/demo/american_journal_of_philology/: 126(1) 2005; five single-author articles in http://muse.jhu.edu/demo/arethusa/: 2005: 38(1); four single-author articles in http://muse.jhu.edu/demo/classical_world/: 2005: 99(1); http://muse.jhu.edu/demo/helios/: 2007: 34(1); nine single-author articles in http://muse.jhu.edu/journals/journal_of_late_antiquity/toc/current.html: 2008: 1(1); two single-author articles in http://muse.jhu.edu/journals/mouseion_journal_of_the_classical_association_of_canada/toc/mou.7.1.html: 2007:7(1); 10 single-author papers in http://muse.jhu.edu/demo/transactions_of_the_american_philological_association/: 2005;135(1); and three single-author papers in http://muse.jhu.edu/demo/hesperia/2005: 71(1). By contrast, there was only a single multiauthored paper in this group: J. C. Kraft, G. Rapp, J. Gifford, and S. Aschenbrenner. 2005. Coastal Change and Archaeological Settings in Eli. *Hesperia* 74: 1–39.

publications cite other secondary sources and often do not cite the primary sources on which our ideas ultimately reside. These publications assume that their readers will either take their conclusions at face value or will have access to extensive research libraries that contain the specialist journals and monographs cited. The authors, their reviewers, and their publishers collectively decided that the benefits of citing primary sources were not worth the cost. General readers would not have access to the primary sources. If they did, they probably would not make the effort to pull them from the shelf. And if they did pull them from the shelf and were able to understand the canonical citation schemes that describe the location of a passage in a text, they would probably not understand what they were looking at. Finally, even if the publishers distributed digital copies of the work on Athenian democracy, the publisher's subscription model would ensure that those publications would reach only those with access to the academic research libraries: many publishers specify that libraries not provide remote access to university alumni and scholars from other, less wealthy institutions.

The top two sites that Google retrieved for "Athenian democracy" in August 2008 were the article in Wikipedia[9] and "Athenian Democracy: A Brief Overview,"[10] from Demos: Classical Athenian Democracy, a book-length and book-like electronic publication on Athenian democracy, largely written by Christopher Blackwell, a classics professor at Furman University, but including labeled publications from other authors as well. While source files are TEI-compliant XML, the form of Demos is entirely traditional: it consists of expository prose and can be downloaded as HTML and PDF.

Two features distinguish the content of Demos from that of its print counterparts. First, Demos is available as an open access publication hosted by the Stoa Publishing Consortium, founded by Ross Scaife in 1997 (and still in operation after its founder's untimely death in March 2008). Second, Demos was composed from the start to exploit the fact that most of the sources about Athenian democracy are freely accessible online as part of the Perseus Digital Library. Demos thus systematically provides links to the primary sources on which its statements about Athenian democracy are based. Demos also includes information about the cultural context and biases of the various Greek sources so that readers will have the background with which to begin critically evaluating the sources on their own. Demos provides a tangible example of how scholarship can substantively exploit the possibilities of the digital medium.

The juxtaposition of Wikipedia and Demos points to one possible way forward in scholarship. We need to combine the immense cultural energy in community-driven projects such as Wikipedia

[9] http://en.wikipedia.org/wiki/Athenian_democracy.

[10] http://www.stoa.org/projects/demos/home.

with the intellectual transparency for which Demos strives.[11] While we will need to develop new ways to evaluate scholarly contributions, classicists at least should have little trouble looking beyond the single-author monograph publication model that now dominates in much of the humanities.[12] Many of us in the field remember when the production of critical editions, scholarly commentaries, and other largely infrastructural projects was still the most prestigious form of publication.

The grand challenges of twenty-first century scholarship reimagine in a digital world the infrastructure that had taken shape to serve the practices of print culture. As early as 1465, Furst and Schoeffer printed Cicero's *De Officiis* and *Paradoxa* in Maintz.[13] After 500 years of continuous scholarly development, print infrastructure for classics had reached a considerable level of maturity. The form of our commentaries, critical editions, lexica, encyclopedias, atlases, and other scholarly tools remained unchanged throughout the twentieth century. Even after the TEI had published conventional methods with which to create genuinely digital editions and geographic information systems had begun to revolutionize the ways in which we visualize space, classicists published print editions and maps. And while some of us were eager to exploit such new methodologies at an early stage, few of us anticipated the immense impact and raw utility that projects such as Wikipedia would exert. The assumptions of print publication had so shaped our thinking that we could not believe that such a radically new form of intellectual production would succeed.

We now face the challenge of rebuilding our infrastructure in a digital form. Much of the intellectual capital that we accumulated in the twentieth century is inaccessible, either because its print format does not lend itself to conversion into a machine-actionable form or because commercial entities own the rights and the content is not available under the open-licensing regimes necessary for eScience in general and ePhilology in particular.[14] Even if we care only about

---

11 Much research has explored how both the Wikipedia model and the data produced by Wikipedia might be useful to the scholarly community. For example see, D. Milne, et al. 2007. A Knowledge-Based Search Engine Powered by Wikipedia. *Proceedings of CIKM 2007*, 445–454; and R. Rosenzweig. 2006. Can History be Open Source?: Wikipedia and the Future of the Past. *Journal of American History* 93(1): 117–146.

12 Indeed there have been a number of recent challenges to the single-author monograph model as well as a call to reshape the entire structure of traditional scholarly communication, for example, see C. Bazerman, et al. 2008. Open Access Book Publishing in Writing Studies: A Case Study. *First Monday* 13(1). Available at http://www.uic.edu/htbin/cgiwrap/bin/ojs/index.php/fm/article/view/2088/1920. See also H. Van de Sompel and C. Lagoze. 2007. Interoperability for the Discovery, Use, and Re-Use of Units of Scholarly Communication. *CTWatch Quarterly* 3(3). Available at http://www.ctwatch.org/quarterly/articles/2007/08/interoperability-for-the-discovery-use-and-re-use-of-units-of-scholarly-communication/.

13 Sandys, J. E. 1908. *A History of Classical Scholarship*, vol. II. Cambridge University Press, 102.

14 For further discussion of this issue, see W. Arms and R. Larsen. 2007. *The Future of Scholarly Communication: Building the Infrastructure for Cyberscholarship*. Report on a NSF-JISC Workshop, April 17–19 2007. Available at http://www.sis.pitt.edu/~repwkshop/SIS-NSFReport2.pdf.

our own research, we need content that can be freely analyzed, visualized, and repurposed. And if we want the ancient world to play the most vigorous possible role in the intellectual life of humanity, we want all the results of our work to be physically and intellectually accessible to the widest-possible audience.

We need to build an infrastructure that provides at least three kinds of access:

- **Access to digital representations of the human record:** This implies providing the best-possible digital representations of our primary data to as many people at as many points on the globe as possible. At this level, we may be delivering a page image from an untranslated Greek text or images associated with some physical location. The term *digital surrogate* is misleading because digital representation such as very high-resolution multispectral scans of manuscripts will often provide more information than would simple access to the physical object.
- **Access to labeled information about the human record:** We should be able to ask for information that is explicitly stated about any named entity: places (e.g., Salamis in Cyprus versus Salamis near Athens); people (Alexander the Great versus the Alexander King of Macedon, who collaborates with Persia in Herodotus); canonical texts citations (e.g., Greek editions, modern language translations, or commentaries that correspond to lines 11–21 of Book I of Homer's *Odyssey*); linguistic phenomena (e.g., the Greek accusative absolute). This level of access essentially (and dramatically) extends the coverage and precision of existing library catalogs, including domain-specific content.
- **Access to automatically generated knowledge:** We can use machine-readable encyclopedias with articles about multiple figures with the same name (e.g., different people named Alexander or different places named Alexandria) to analyze the content of these articles for clues with which to determine which of these Alexanders or Alexandrias particular passages in classical texts probably denote. We can use machine-readable dictionaries and modern language translations aligned to Greek and Latin source texts to determine the meaning of a particular word in an untranslated passage (e.g., does Latin *orationes* correspond to English "prayers," "speeches," or something else in a given passage?). We can use Treebanks (databases that track the syntactic relations of words in a sentence: e.g., word *X* is the main verb, with word *Y* as its subject and word *Z* as its object) to train parsers that can then begin decoding the syntactic structure of sentences for which no parses exist. We can use models of a user's educational background (e.g., the vocabulary of every Greek text and the textbooks on ancient Greek history they have studied in their coursework) to predict new words and concepts in a given passage and then to rank these new words and concepts by importance according to various criteria.

Our ultimate goal must be to make the full record of humanity accessible to every human being, regardless of linguistic and cultural background. In this, we expand upon the recurrent and obviously impractical idea of capturing the sum of human knowledge. Similarly chimerical impulses surely were at work in the Aristotelian school of fourth-century BCE Athens, the great library of Alexandria in the third century, the entrepreneurial printers of Europe in the late fifteenth century, and German classicists of the nineteenth century, just as similar dreams move projects such as the Open Content Alliance (OCA) and Google Books in our time. The impracticality of these impulses served the very practical purpose of helping each of these projects envision a radically different world and leave the world different, indeed better, than they found it.[15]

The universal library represents an unattainable point of reference: it is like a star toward which we navigate. If we face in this direction, we can flesh out the twists and turns of navigable paths toward distant but attainable goals. For our group, the goal is to make the core information about the classical world accessible to speakers of every major European language and of Chinese and Arabic. The European Union has a fundamental mission to serve its own language communities and has made an ongoing investment in multilingual technologies.[16] The United States Government, by contrast, identified Arabic and Chinese as strategic languages. Corporations such as Google, Yahoo, and Microsoft serve global audiences and have major needs for multilingual systems. Classicists can organize their labor to build upon these larger infrastructural efforts.

There are three major strategies to make a growing core of information about the Greco-Roman world accessible to audiences in a range of languages and cultures.

- **Domain optimization for machine translation**: General systems for machine translation, translation support, cross-language information retrieval, and other multilingual services attempt to do a reasonable job on any category of input, but in so doing, they cannot make simplifying assumptions about the text on which they are working. In effect, we create language models for representative corpora about Greek and Latin. Such language models would reflect the fact that a term such as *case* probably describes a linguistic category (e.g., accusative or dative case) in a grammatical text but not a display cabinet in a museum catalog. A preprocessor could label most likely translations for those terms whose meanings diverge most in a given text from more-general language models. Such an approach requires training data for each source

[15] Much has been written comparing the different models of the OCA and Google Books. See R. K. Johnson. 2007. In Google's Broad Wake: Taking Responsibility for Shaping the Global Digital Library. *ARL: A Bimonthly Report on Research Library Issues and Actions from ARL, CNI, and SPARC*, 1–17; and O. Y. Rieger. 2008. *Preservation in the Age of Large-Scale Digitization*. Washington, D. C.: Council on Library and Information Resources. Available at http://www.clir.org/pubs/reports/pub141/pub141.pdf.

[16] For an example of this work in terms of digital libraries, see M. Agosti, et al. 2007. Roadmap for Multilingual Information Access in the European Library. *Proceedings of ECDL 2007*, 136–147.

language (in classics, English, French, German, and Italian as a start). Such training sets may require substantial labor to establish but they can be applied to open-ended bodies of semantically coherent text.

- **Maximizing the amount of basic data stored in ontologies and other abstract formats:** Ontologies can rapidly become complex and idiosyncratic, but if we concentrate on basic propositional statements from mature conceptual reference models (e.g., TEI P5,[17] CIDOC CRM,[18] FRBRoo[19]), we can create knowledge bases that are much easier to convert into multiple languages than is full text. The ontological categories should allow systems to apply the classics language models even more effectively than in more general text (i.e., systems will have much better data with which to determine whether they are viewing museum catalog entries or a grammatical database when they confront terms such as *case*).
- **Exploiting detailed linguistic annotations on canonical texts:** Perseus has already published the first 50,000 words of a Latin Treebank, representing the syntax of each sentence as a tree structure and thus addressing one major category of ambiguity that causes problems in machine translation.[20] Work continues on the Latin Treebank, and Perseus has just received funding to begin work on a million-word Treebank for classical Greek. Other forms of annotation allow us to resolve additional classes of ambiguity (e.g., a co-reference annotation would allow us to indicate that a pronoun such as *hic* refers to Cicero rather than Caesar). Digital editions may devote more energy to linguistic annotations of this kind than to the traditional revision of textual readings in frequently edited texts. We should design these annotations to facilitate accurate translation into multiple languages. The annotations being keyed to Greek and Latin are, in fact, another form of propositional knowledge and should be useful to anyone reading Greek and Latin, whether they are native speakers of Arabic and Chinese or of English and German.

In producing a digital infrastructure for their field, classicists find themselves engaged again in the most established scholarly practices of their field: the production of editions, lexica, commentaries, encyclopedias, grammars, and other scholarly tools. In the digital world, however, these tools are no longer static objects but dynamic systems that can interact with each other and with their human readers. These books begin to answer Plato's criticism that writing could not answer the questions posed by its readers. Classicists are now in a position to begin new research projects that were not feasible in print culture. Even more important, classicists can now expand the role that their field plays, not only in Europe and North

17 http://www.tei-c.org/Guidelines/P5/.

18 http://cidoc.ics.forth.gr/.

19 http://cidoc.ics.forth.gr/docs/frbr_oo/frbr_docs/FRBR_oo_V0.9.pdf.

20 http://nlp.perseus.tufts.edu/syntax/treebank/.

America but also in intellectual communities with ancient classical traditions (such as the Islamic world) and in which Greco-Roman culture can figure with more prominence than was ever feasible before (such as China and India). Classicists—and all humanists—have an opportunity to develop a new, global intellectual culture that transcends the boundaries of the past.

The Changing Landscape of American Studies in a Global Era

Caroline Levander

Introduction and State of the Field

What is the future of American Studies in a global era? Does it make intellectual sense to retain the national referent of "American" as an organizing system of knowledge at the current moment, and is there something identifiable as American in an increasingly global culture? American Studies emerged as a distinct multidisciplinary research field during the Cold War, and its intellectual assumptions, some argue, have tended to be bounded by the era's incipient nationalism. Yet the field's founding limitation—brought into stark relief in the current global moment—has actually generated one of the most significant intellectual opportunities in humanities scholarship in recent history.

How might we conceptualize American Studies research once we pry it loose from the geographic assumptions that have so long defined it and that reinforce the notion of a uniform, "united" nation or state? What happens to our research tools and techniques once we put pressure on the "American" part of the terminology used to designate American Studies as a distinct object of inquiry? These are the questions that are currently reconstituting how scholars undertake research across the fields of American literature, American history, and American religious studies.

Over the past two decades, interdisciplinary work that moves beyond analysis of any one nation in isolation and that places urgent intellectual questions in the larger matrix of the Americas as a hemisphere has begun to assume prominence across humanities and social science disciplines. New graduate and undergraduate programs at institutions such as the University of Southern California, Indiana University, and the University of Toronto; new journals such as *Comparative American Literature* and *Review of International American Studies;* and new associations such as the International American Studies

Association mark a dramatic shift in focus away from nation-based frameworks. Remarkable new possibilities for Americanist study are opened up when "America" is understood not as a synonym for an isolated nation but as a network of cultural influences that have extended across the hemisphere from the period of colonization to the present. Clearly, future research and curricula on all regions of the Americas will increasingly emphasize comparative and cross-regional studies.

This seismic shift in the field imaginary has generated an unprecedented need for innovative research tools and methods. Scholars are faced with the challenge of finding new ways of doing research as well as new objects of study. We must create nimble and interactive communities of scholarly inquiry that reflect hemispheric studies' essential dynamism—communities that allow us to develop new research methods that emerge out of an understanding that national boundaries are overlapping and multiform rather than fixed. The traditional humanities research model of single-author books is giving way to collaborative research that is being undertaken by scholars who recognize that hemispheric studies work requires collaborative ventures across diverse fields of expertise. Increasingly, multiauthor books and articles, as well as grant proposals by scholars working in this interdisciplinary field, are challenging longstanding models of humanistic academic achievement. These collaborative research ventures are slowly transforming how humanities research is conceived. In the next decade, more new communities, methods, and tools are sure to emerge to meet the challenges and opportunities that a hemispheric studies approach affords.

The transition from a national to a hemispheric American Studies promises to reinvigorate existing fields. At the same time, however, it poses a serious challenge to received models of intellectual training, research, disciplinarity, and curriculum development. Although many now recognize the importance of this transformation, there is scant existing infrastructure for researchers who want to conceive their intellectual work within the rubric of this new research area. Archives, universities, academic presses, and federal funding agencies tend to reinforce national research communities, to organize knowledge within national rubrics, and therefore to inadvertently circumscribe the very questions that scholars seek to address. New learning communities, research tools, and methods are therefore urgently needed for those scholars interested in developing hemispheric learning communities.

Research Potential

Innovative digital environments, resources, services, and infrastructure are essential to the success of this new research field. In fact, rich digital media are uniquely suited to address the challenges and opportunities of reconstituting American Studies through hemispheric, transnational approaches for the following reasons.

First, the amount of data sorting that researchers must do necessitates greater flexibility across knowledge and textual fields. Scholars trained as Mexicanists, U.S. Americanists, or Brazilianists can manipulate national archives to conduct nation-based research, but these research skills and data fields are insufficient for research that endeavors to engage multinational and transnational contexts. The sheer amount of material defies traditional research methods, even as the intellectual focus of the research makes nation-focused archives and nation-organized search engines largely irrelevant.

Second, the shift from nation-based to hemispheric research models requires the development of new research tools that simultaneously capture spatial and temporal data. Geographic areas become dynamic, fluid, and multilayered research fields from a hemispheric perspective. Likewise strict, linear narratives of modern development—be they historical, anthropological, literary, religious, sociological, biological, or economic—fail to capture the multidimensional, multidirectional, and palimpsestic nature of hemispheric research. New tools that enable researchers to explore spatial and temporal dynamism are essential to hemispheric studies scholarship.

Third, this new scholarship requires the creation of an interactive research community that focuses on the overlapping histories of the states and nations of the Americas from the vantage point of a hemispheric, rather than a nation-bound, academic environment. The effort of many U.S. universities to internationalize by establishing satellite campuses expands institutional reach but fails to create a truly transnational scholarly climate. By creating a virtual world that overcomes barriers of time, space, language, economic, and cultural difference, digital media specialists and hemispheric studies scholars can transform graduate education and faculty collaboration by creating a transnational research culture. Functioning as a hemispheric university that is sustained and enhanced not by annual conference attendance and scholarly publications (as now tends to be the case) but by ongoing, interactive virtual engagement, such a community has the potential to create intellectual environments not bounded by disciplinary tradition, national culture, and monolingual norms.

Fourth, a hemispheric studies method requires dramatic pedagogical innovation at every level of teaching. The study of history, literature, and languages has been partitioned into national categories, and existing teaching tools assume the stability and inevitability of national borders. Innovative geographic models are beginning to replace categories of national literature and history with transnational rubrics such as the Pacific Rim, the transatlantic, the formerly colonized world, or the Black Atlantic. Yet the questions remain: How does one teach the Americas? How do courses with traditional U.S. foci (U.S. literature survey and U.S. history survey, for example) engage other, often lost or marginalized stories? What different technologies are needed when these stories become part of our teaching toolbox? How do research databases address the challenges of multilingualism that an Americas approach raises? Is it possible to teach the more complex, multilayered, and often-obscured literary, religious, and social histories of the Americas given existing institutional and curricular constraints? These questions confront teachers at all levels, and answering them will necessitate increasingly rich digital environments. Students' ability to manipulate innovative digital media can offset their tendency toward monolingualism and can serve as a bridge between cultural worlds.

Rich Digital Environments: Archives and Learning Contexts

As is now probably quite clear, one of the most daunting research challenges for Americas scholars is the archive itself. Primary research material has been sifted, sorted, and processed in ways that obscure and impede non-nation-based inquiry. From subject headings to search terms to national archives, extant humanities knowledge has been organized around the idea of nation, state, or area as homologous entity. Yet, as scholars from Jacques Derrida (*Archive Fever*, 1996) to Carolyn Steedman (*Dust: The Archive and Cultural History*, 2001) have observed, archives are far from objective repositories of knowledge.

To complicate matters even further, the history of print has always been in close relationship with the history of nationalism in Western culture. This relationship began in the fifteenth century, and at least since the eighteenth century, Western print culture has traditionally reinforced the importance of the nation-state as the default frame of literary and historical reference. What, how, and why certain documents are published and others are not therefore reflects particular cultural pressures and expectations. Still today, widely disseminated historical collections and literary anthologies tend to include those materials that uphold, rather than complicate, national paradigms. In short, most aspects of producing and archiving print matter militate against organizing knowledge differently. Once we recognize the extent to which print and archive cultures can collectively work to shore up strategic ways of conceptualizing the past and present, we can begin to see the profound importance that innovative digital archives might have for Americas scholarship.

Digital archives can offer new opportunities for rethinking the nation-state as the organizing rubric for literary and cultural history of the Americas. The digital medium offers unique opportunities for a hemispheric approach to historical and literary analysis in two important ways. First, because digital archives can be published not for profit, they are free to bring together materials irrespective of cost or profit from throughout the Americas, including, but not limited to, the U.S. American nation-state, as well as rare texts and texts in the original language that offer a new level of access for research and pedagogy. The second key advantage of the digital over the print medium is the former's potential for international access and scholarly collaboration as well as editorial partnership. A digital archive can reach an international audience of scholars, researchers, and students who may not otherwise have access to documents housed in U.S. archives or to published materials. Unlike the print medium, the digital medium makes possible an unprecedented level of editorial collaboration through hypertextual cross-referencing in cyberspace. Because digital archives make available materials that are dispersed in different geographic locations, the archives facilitate collaboration and intellectual exchange among an international audience.

In short, the digital medium offers rich opportunities for transnational exchange and is therefore uniquely suited for a hemispheric approach to history. These observations are no doubt already familiar to many, but they are worth emphasizing because digital archives have the potential to radically reconceive the organizing premises of stored knowledge and to make hidden texts, material, and pasts immediately apparent.

One example of such an archive is the Our Americas Archive Partnership, or OAAP (http://oaap.rice.edu/). This collaboration between Rice University (Houston, Texas), University of Maryland, and Instituto Mora (Mexico City) was funded in 2007 by a three-year National Leadership Grant from the Institute of Museum and Library Services. The project brings together Americas-focused archival material from all three institutions in order to innovate both information science and academic research. Two online collections of materials in English and Spanish—the Early Americas Digital Archive (EADA) at University of Maryland and a new digital archive of materials being developed at Rice with Mora—provide an initial corpus for testing the tools. The multilingual archives illustrate the complex politics and histories that characterize the American hemisphere, but they also provide unique opportunities to further digital research in the humanities. Geographic visualization, as well as new social tagging and tag cloud cluster models, are just some of the interface techniques that the OAAP will develop with the goal of creating innovative research pathways. Users will have geospatial search, social tagging, and faceted-browsing tools to aid their manipulation of multilingual documents focusing on the Americas from the late fifteenth to the early twentieth century. As a result, new research themes, such as the contingency of nation formation, the unpredictability of national histories, and the protean character of the nation itself, come into view. New political and cultural relationships along and across national borders emerge. Translations and transcriptions of handwritten documents will make the broad range of documents more accessible to diverse audiences. The OAAP aims to innovate information science as well as academic research, and its open source technological infrastructure and interface will provide an important model for other digital library projects. Because the architecture supports integration of multiple repositories without the need of a common repository infrastructure, OAAP is meant to promote collaboration with other digital libraries. The goal is to gradually reorganize knowledge and access to material relevant to the Americas in such a way as to encourage innovation by scholars and digital media specialists across the Americas.

With these kinds of digital archives as one of their features, new research environments can become an important next step in developing a vitalized, fully realized hemispheric studies research climate. They will allow us to envision the shape, texture, and contours of the Americas over time and space: what it looked like, how it developed and changed, and why some parts of its story are dominant while others are not. They will allow us to produce, as well as to absorb, knowledge collaboratively. They will generate new questions about disciplinary practices and humanistic study, not only as they get institutionalized through study of the territory comprising the Americas but also as they confront new opportunities and limits in a global economy.

Embedding rich archives like the OAAP, such a new research environment or collaboratory, for example, might focus on building an urban environment (replete with amphitheater, classrooms, exhibit space for interactive research, lectures that take different aspects of the hemisphere as their focus, and new search tools) that facilitates transnational collaborative research. Rather than having to overcome the boundaries—be they cultural, national, linguistic, disciplinary, or institutional—that separate distinct learning communities across the hemisphere, such an environment could focus on what a truly transnational learning environment would look like. It could ask questions such as, What research opportunities emerge once academic collaboration occurs within the primary context of the hemisphere rather than the nation? What new methods and technologies best generate rigorous and innovative research in this growing field of hemispheric studies? What happens when researchers' learning environment as well as their object of study becomes transnational and hemispheric? By developing new methods of research as well as new objects of study, such a research collaboratory would create a new, interactive community of scholarly inquiry and constitute a collaborative and transnational research environment. It would function as a sort of hemispheric university—generating new research and learning models that develop out of a transnational scholarly climate.

Through visualization of diverse archival records—for example, linguistic maps, population records, regional religions, agricultural data, climatological change records, and archaeological information on migration and settlement—such an information-rich environment would allow users to develop a deeply contextual and multiperspective framework for formulating ambitious questions and research projects. Bringing into synergistic engagement ways of knowing that are often isolated by disciplinary method, such an environment has the potential to transform how humanities does its work—the questions it asks, the goals it sets for itself, and the disciplinary order it generates.

Conclusion

New research communities are springing up to meet the needs of an emerging field of inquiry in the Americas. The challenge to rethink the field's intellectual premises within the context of new geopolitical formations has generated a renaissance in scholarship in American Studies. While outstanding universities and scholars are producing innovative research and new book series are providing critical venues for scholarship that capture this shift in intellectual perspective, little attention has been paid to the overarching methodological, institutional, and pedagogical issues resulting from the growth of inter-American or American hemispheric studies. The oversight is unfortunate because this scholarly paradigm shift challenges us to reconsider almost every assumption that we have as humanists. From data collection and archivization to scholarly dissemination and pedagogical practices to how we organize humanistic knowledge and the questions we can imagine asking, the turn to Americas scholarship has put pressure on the very terms in which we work as humanists. Given the nature of these pressures—exponential increases in material that scholars need to process and challenges to the intellectual coordinates we use to orient ourselves, to name only a few—rich digital resources, innovative technical infrastructures, and new tools are essential if we are to ask the questions that matter and find the answers that will stand the tests of time and space.

A Whirlwind Tour of Automated Language Processing for the Humanities and Social Sciences

Douglas W. Oard

Abstract

Automating some types of language processing holds great promise for helping us develop new ways of drawing insight from the world's linguistic legacy. But "promise" has many meanings, and this is a promise that has not yet been kept. This essay outlines the structure of the relevant disciplines, briefly describes the process by which automated language processing systems are created, and then offers some suggestions for how systems that better meet the needs of humanities and social science scholars might be built.

Introduction

We find ourselves at the threshold of a new era. Behind us is an era of almost entirely manual markup and transcription; ahead we envision increasing reliance on automation for at least the more mundane parts of that work. We regularly hear impressive claims for what future technology—always, it seems, *future* technology—will be able to do for us. Why is this future perpetually just over the horizon? The reason, I argue, is simple: those who could build these marvels don't really understand what marvels we need, and we, who understand what we need all too well, don't really understand what can be built. So we find ourselves in a situation a bit like the one depicted in the old cartoon of a blind person ringing the doorbell at the school for the deaf: we need new ways of communicating. Learning more about the other folks is a good way to start any process of communication, so in this brief essay I'll share a few of the things I have learned in my time among system builders. The situation is really quite simple: they are organized as tribes, they work their magic using models (rather like voodoo), they worship the word *maybe*, and they never do anything right the first time.

The Many Tribes of Language Processing

We seem to lack the right vocabulary for talking about this subject. Some refer to the broad subject as "text mining"—a term that has been used in so many incompatible ways that it may be better suited to marketing than to research. The core challenge here is social rather than technical: research communities form in ways that tend to balkanize the intellectual space. Rather than fight it, let's go with the flow and look at these communities in the ways that they think of themselves.

As a first step, it would be helpful to say a word about the four forms of human language. Four? Yes, four. Spoken language, written language, and sign language probably immediately come to mind. But what's the fourth? It is character-coded language, by which I mean what some call e-text: digital representation of individual characters (for example, English text represented as a sequence of ASCII characters). While this is indeed just another form of writing, the distinction is an important one because other forms of human language must generally be converted into character-coded text before we can easily manipulate their content. This distinction then serves to define two very active conversion communities: document image processing and speech processing. (Automatic transcription of sign language is not yet nearly as well developed.)

Like me, you probably grew up referring to document image processing as "OCR." Optical character recognition (OCR) is indeed an important part of the process, but it is just one piece of a complex pipeline that starts with what might generally be termed "layout analysis." The goal of layout analysis is to reconstruct the logical structure of a document. You might think of this as an attempt to recover the structural markup from which the document could have been generated. This is usually a three-stage process: (1) detect the physical structure (e.g., where on the page was that handwritten annotation made?); (2) classify each item using meaningful categories (e.g., logo, salutation, or body text); and (3) infer the logical structure from the available evidence (e.g., use relative position to guess which part of the text a handwritten annotation refers to). As you can see from this example, document image processing is about more than recognizing the correct sequence of printed characters: we need to handle handwriting, logos, structural elements such as tables and captions, and quite a challenging set of inferences about the author's (or annotator's) intent. As we will see again below, issues beyond mere content are also sometimes important. Can we tell from the style of the handwriting who wrote this note? Can we reliably determine what type of document this is (a form? a business letter? a memorandum? a page from a book?). All these problems are familiar to humanities scholars. If only they were equally familiar to our OCR programs how much easier our lives might be. Researchers who work on this gather each January at the Document Recognition and Retrieval Conference in San Jose, California. If you want to study document image processing engineers in their natural habitat, that's the place to be.

Similarly, speech processing involves far more than the "automatic speech recognition" (ASR) that we all have heard about. There are essentially three subcommunities within speech processing: (1) interactive voice response systems (like the ones that answer the phone when you call an airline); (2) individually trained dictation systems, which were the first system to reach the market; and (3) systems that are still in the research lab. Research systems will be of greatest interest to us, since applications such as transcribing interviews, meetings, or streaming media require that we be able to accommodate a great deal of variability. Often the first step is to automatically figure out who spoke when, which goes by the unfortunate name "diarization." Once we know that, then transcriptions can be automatically adapted to do as well as possible on each speaker. This is followed by disfluency repair (e.g., to get the "umms" out) and then by (also infelicitously named) "pretty printing" techniques that guess where to insert sentence boundaries and capitalization and that try to convert spoken numbers to a reasonable written form. Speech processing researchers can be found each year at the International Conference on Acoustics, Speech and Signal Processing (ICASSP).

You might think that completes our discussion of conversion since now we have character-coded text, but you would be wrong. A third important type of conversion is paraphrase: automating the conversion of one expression of a set of ideas in character-coded text to another expression of those same ideas. (Thankfully, intentionally changing the ideas usually still requires human involvement!) Two forms of paraphrase are of particular importance: summarization and machine translation. In summarization, we seek to express some part of the ideas more succinctly. So-called *extractive* summarization techniques do this by simply selecting some parts of the text to show you—Google search results are one familiar example. You'll be disappointed to learn that that's pretty close to the state of the art—which provides some measure of job security for the people who write abstracts, I suppose. Summarization researchers can be found at the Text Analysis Conference (TAC), held each year in Gaithersburg, Maryland.

The other key type of paraphrase, *machine translation* (MT), works essentially like a translating parrot: the machine "hears" one language and tries to parrot back those ideas using words from another language. Because different languages might put their words in a different order, this is a really challenging problem that keeps MT researchers up late at night. As anyone who has used one of the many free Web translation services knows, the results are sometimes more useful for their humor than for the elegance of their expression: nuance is not the machine's long suit. You can study machine-translation researchers in the wild (along with their friends from natural language processing) at the annual conference of the Association for Computational Linguistics.

In some sense, all of this is natural language processing (NLP), but rather early on that moniker got appropriated by the people interested in telling nouns and verbs apart (remember diagramming sentences during your grammar school days?). Over the years, the NLP community (who also call their field "computational linguistics," which has a bit more of an academic ring to it) grew to embrace several large-scale problems, including summarization and MT. Three others are particularly noteworthy: extraction, classification, and clustering.

Extraction is the problem of identifying spans of text that are important for some purpose. The canonical example in NLP is to find proper names (e.g., names of people) in newspaper stories. But it doesn't take too great a leap of imagination to realize that we might use similar techniques to at least partially annotate much of what we call "coding" in the social sciences, i.e., labeling the things that our informants say with our interpretation of their meaning. This requires that we combine extraction with the second key capability: classification. The canonical classification problem is that I show you 100 newspaper stories and I tell you the category to which each belongs (international news, finance, sports, etc.). I then show you story number 101, and you decide which category it should be assigned to. When extraction and classification are combined (now classifying the span of text, not the entire story) the result is called "tagging" (which is unfortunately confusable with the more recently introduced idea of "social tagging," in which we trick ordinary people into doing a similar kind of work for us). Showing the machine all those examples is a bother, so clustering, the third key capability, tries to avoid that by just assuming that things that are similar should be labeled in the same way. Of course, that doesn't tell you what the label should be, but extraction might help with that (just extract whatever words seem to be most strongly associated with the cluster and hope for the best).

As this brief description has illustrated, these three capabilities can be put together in different ways for different purposes. Some well-known examples are authorship attribution (a type of nontopical classification), duplicate detection (a restricted form of clustering), and creation of a concordance (which is simply clustering text spans that share a common term). There are, therefore, many reasons why hanging out with NLP folks can be a good use of your time.

The black sheep of the NLP family is information retrieval (IR), which is a fancy name for what the rest of us call "search engines." IR and NLP developed as separate fields because they initially had little in common; IR folks just want to build useful systems without worrying too much about linguistics, while NLP folks start with linguistics and work toward useful systems. The two communities have much in common, and indeed you can find work on classification and clustering in both places. But search engines never did get subsumed into NLP, so you'll need to go to an IR conference if you want to hear the latest about searching. Interestingly, the IR community itself is somewhat bifurcated, with the IR systems folks hanging out with each other at the annual conference of the Association for Computing Machinery (ACM) Special Interest Group on Information

Retrieval (SIGIR) and the human-centered side of the field most in evidence at the annual conference of the American Society for Information Science and Technology (which is not really as U.S.-centric as it sounds, but it makes for a clever acronym).

What can we conclude from this techno-smorgasbord? One fairly obvious conclusion is that we need to find ways to communicate across disciplines about what is needed and what can be built. When such disparate worlds meet and try to communicate, they often select "boundary objects" that both can understand. In this case, we call that boundary object "metadata," and that is where we next turn our attention.

Mastering Their Voodoo

We are ambivalent about our metadata. People often misunderstand "ambivalent" as expressing a lack of preference; more properly, it means that something possesses both good points and bad points. Indeed, that's a reasonable summary of how many people feel about metadata. We like metadata because it allows us to get at meaning and the context in which that meaning arises, not merely at how that meaning was expressed in some specific case. Builders of language technology would say the same thing by observing that metadata allows us to go beyond the "surface form" to expose "latent variables": that way of saying it better fits their way of thinking about "models" that contain "variables." But metadata introduces its own problems; among the most frequently mentioned are cost and consistency. Interestingly, technologists are not nearly as bothered by these problems as we are, in part because they already understand that what we are trying to do is impossible.

OK, that's a pretty strong claim, so it probably merits a bit of discussion before we go on. Two factors combine to prevent us from creating perfectly accurate metadata. First, we don't always know for sure what the texts we are working with really mean. Second, we don't always know for sure what the metadata that we are creating really means. Solve those two problems, and this would be easy.

But the issue is not that we don't know how to solve these problems; it is that we know they *can't* be solved. Let's start with the question of what a text means. Language is a human creation, and language use is a creative act. Indeed, it is our ability to reason in the presence of ambiguity that makes it possible for us to express new ideas using an existing language. But wait, you say, isn't well-structured metadata supposed to allow for that? Here we meet the second problem: we simply can't agree on what we mean by our metadata. Consider a very well-standardized classification scheme, perhaps one that could be applied to this paper. Then run a quick thought experiment: train 1,000 indexers to classify essays like this one without showing them this paper. You know full well that no matter how well they are trained, and no matter how careful they are, some of the indexers will disagree with others about how this essay should be classified. The reason for this disagreement is not something that we can change, because the true meaning of our metadata exists only in our minds. Assignment of metadata is always an expression of an opinion rather than a statement of fact. Since people naturally will sometimes hold different opinions, our metadata is bound to exhibit some degree of inconsistency.

These same problems plagued NLP researchers for decades because NLP was originally conceived of as first encoding meaning in ways that people could understand, and then using that encoded meaning to do something useful. Starting in the 1980s (and with roots that go back further than that), a group of young turks in the NLP world decided to simply stop worrying about all this and learn to love uncertainty. When asked whether statement *A* has meaning *B*, they would always answer "maybe," and then work some wizardry with probability theory to figure out just how likely it was to be true. This proved to be a bit of a niche industry in the NLP business until some of the young turks demonstrated an MT system that did as well as the best existing systems by using statistics with only three facts: spaces separate words, periods end sentences, and an awful lot of examples of what good translations look like are available. It was this third fact that changed everything. When examples of language use were scarce, the human ability to see broad patterns from a few examples provided a useful foundation for NLP. But once computational access to language became ubiquitous, the ability of the machine to identify and memorize exceptions rapidly outpaced human abilities. And this is what made it possible for probability theory—the "science of maybe"—to come to the fore. Indeed, the transformation has been so complete that statistical modeling now lies at the core of every one of the disciplines identified in the previous section.

This tectonic shift has two important implications for us: we must learn new ways of thinking about what we are doing (generating and using metadata) and how we are doing it (using computational models). Jeannette Wing, who directs computer science research at the National Science Foundation, refers to this as "computational thinking," and she claims that it can be good for you regardless of whether you have any interest in computers. Let's take this one piece at a time, starting with computational modeling.

The word *model* is usually defined as a representation of some aspect of reality. Computational models often focus on behaviors, specifying how some input is related to some output (the classifiers mentioned earlier are one example of this). Over the years, the document image processing, speech processing, NLP, and IR communities converged on what is generally referred to as an "evaluation-guided research paradigm." The key idea here is that they start by identifying some challenge problem (e.g., a set of newspaper stories and a set of category labels to be assigned to those stories), an answer key (a "correct" set of assignments), and an evaluation measure (e.g., what fraction of the system's assignments are "right"). The programmer then goes off and designs a system that does the job, albeit not perfectly. After seeing the results, the programmers go back to the lab, try to build a better system, and again examine the results. They repeat this process until they run out of ideas. Because these systems are just trying different ways of learning the associated probabilities, the process can be partly automated, and it is not uncommon for developers to try a hundred, or even a thousand, variants of their system design overnight. This process has proven to be remarkably effective, but it has one key weakness: if the developers can't measure it, they can't improve it. So the entire process turns on how the challenge problem, the answer key, and the evaluation measure are constructed. The good news is that scholars in the humanities and social sciences don't need to learn probability theory to help guide this process. But we do need to start creating challenge problems, answer keys, and evaluation measures that reflect what we actually need the technology to do. So find someone who does this kind of research and ask that person to describe the challenge problems that they're presently working on. You'll be appalled by how far those "canned problems" are from what we really need. No wonder this stuff doesn't work well for us yet: the developers of the technology we need are not yet asking the right questions.

The bad news, however, is that humanities scholars are going to need to learn a bit of probability theory (many social scientists will have a leg up there). The reason for this comes back to the weakness in our boundary object—the way we think about metadata. When we've asked, "What metadata should be assigned here?" we have really meant, "What is the probability distribution over possible values for the metadata that should be assigned here?" We just didn't know that's what we meant. I am realistic enough to realize that we are not all going to go out and study probability theory just so that we can understand what all those computer scientists are saying. In the near term, this is why we need to work in interdisciplinary teams, learning from each other. But just as the children of "digital immigrants" grow up today to be "digital natives," our graduate students will grow up in a brave new world in which the answer to every question is "maybe" (assuming that they can keep a straight face with us long enough to pass their dissertation defense). So when I say that we need to learn probability theory, I don't really mean you and me—I mean our students. But nothing could be more natural; we merely need to shape the world in which they can do it.

Getting It Right

Peter Drucker once observed that the best way to predict the future is to create it. So let me close this essay with a few thoughts on what I think we should do.

- *Build useful tools, but don't try to automate the intellectual work of scholars.* This may seem obvious, but that hasn't stopped people before who have tried to build machines that do things we don't yet understand.
- *Dream big.* It is tempting to think about how best to use what we can already do (as the many studies that we already have that are

based simply on counting words amply illustrate). But real progress will come from the intersection between envisioning what we need and understanding what can be built. We're not going to get there if we keep starting with what has already been built. The key to the future is what we can model, not merely what we can see.

- *Waste money wisely*. After people landed on the moon, the phrase "it's not rocket science" entered our lexicon as a way of explaining that something wasn't really as hard as it might seem to be. But the challenge we face is not rocket science: it is harder than rocket science. After all, rocket scientists know what they are trying to do; they just need to figure out how to do it. We, by contrast, need some way of learning about what we are really trying to do. I used to work for the chief of naval research, who once said in a speech, "I am the only admiral in the Navy who can be wrong 90 percent of the time and keep my job." Why? Fundamentally, because technology researchers don't really know what it is they are trying to do. So initially (and, quite often, repeatedly), they do the wrong thing. The good ones learn as they go, and in the end they do some right thing, even if it was not really what they were trying to do in the first place. Essentially, this is the culture of the inventor, and it is one that we would do well to learn a bit more about. This may be our most challenging cultural shift, but it is one that we must make if we are going to make progress for one simple reason: metadata is not the right boundary object. The natural boundary object around which to build a conversation about what can be built is the system that creates that metadata.
- *Don't reinvent the wheel*. When you come down to it, statistical language processing is all about learning from examples. When people started thinking this way, it was natural to start by hand-building examples. For example, when people wanted to automate the process of drawing sentence diagrams (which they call "parsing"), they hired a slew of people to spend a few years generating some sentence diagrams that their machines could learn from. The leading edge these days, by contrast, is focused on taking advantage of examples that already exist. For example, when Ed Hovy wanted examples of good summaries for a week's worth of newspaper stories, he looked to a weekly newsmagazine. What does this have to do with us? Well, we have been building examples of what we need for some time. The trick is to think of the things that we have already marked up as "training data." Just tell someone who works on statistical language processing that you have heaps of training data already created for a new problem that is of great importance to our society. A sure ticket to instant popularity.
- *Make friends*. We're like yin and yang: we have the problem and they have the solution, so we need to find ways to work together. As a first step, there are now workshops at some of the conferences mentioned above that often go by names like "Cultural Heritage Applications of Language Processing." That's a springboard that could ultimately lead to formation of project teams, but only

> if we start going to their workshops (or they start coming to ours). Our European colleagues are ahead of us here: they've been putting money on the table to support interdisciplinary project teams that will work together for a few years on a specific problem. Of course, we do some of that in the United States as well—perhaps fewer teams, but sometimes with more resources per team. This is a natural approach, but we should think of it as a means to an end rather than as the end in itself. The byproduct of projects like this is a new cohort of doctoral students who will be the "natives" in this new world. The first generation of our young turks is already in place, and that will make the path that much easier for the next generation. These students are without question our future. Dan Goldin, a former administrator of National Aeronautics and Space Administration (NASA), had a mantra of "faster, better, cheaper." Ultimately, NASA decided that it could have any two of the three, but not all three, and today someone else runs NASA. But Goldin's idea was the right one: if you change the way you think, you can sometimes get all three. And the shift from interdisciplinary teams to interdisciplinary scholars will likely be such a transition. Nothing we could do is more important than educating the next generation of scholars to work at this intersection.

For many years, our technology colleagues have built provocative demonstrations of what they can accomplish. That is the "field of dreams" approach, and it is the only practical place to start: if they build it, (maybe) we will come. The ball is in our court.

Acknowledgments

This work was supported in part by National Science Foundation awards IIS-0122466 (MALACH) and IIS-0729459 (PopIT). I am grateful to my colleagues on both projects for the opportunity to learn from them, but they will be pleased to learn that the opinions expressed here are mine alone.

Information Visualization: Challenge for the Humanities

Maureen Stone

Digital archiving creates a vast store of knowledge that can be accessed only through digital tools. Users of this information will need fluency in the tools of digital access, exploration, visualization, analysis, and collaboration. This paper proposes that this fluency represents a new form of literacy, which must become fundamental for humanities scholars.

Tools influence both the creation and the analysis of information. Whether using pen and paper, Microsoft Office, or Web 2.0, scholars base their process, production, and questions on the capabilities their tools offer them. Digital archiving and the interconnectivity of the Web provide new challenges in terms of quantity and quality of information. They create a new medium for presentation as well as a foundation for collaboration that is independent of physical location. Challenges for digital humanities include:

- developing new genres for complex information presentation that can be shared, analyzed, and compared;
- creating a literacy in information analysis and visualization that has the same rigor and richness as current scholarship; and
- expanding classically text-based pedagogy to include simulation, animation, and spatial and geographic representation.

Information in digital form provides unequalled opportunity to combine, distill, present, and share complex ideas. The challenge is to do so in a way that balances complexity with conciseness, and accuracy with essence, that speaks authoritatively, yet inspires exploration and personal insight. This presentation goes beyond illustrated texts organized as pages, or even as Web pages, to include interactive graphical representations based on data.

While literacy in all new media will be crucial for digital scholarship of the future, this paper focuses on *information visualization,* or the creation of graphical representations of data that harness the pattern-recognition skills of the human visual system. The skills that support information visualization include data analysis, visual design, and an understanding of human perception and cognition.

As my specific expertise is color, I will include both the use of color in visualization and the visualization of color in art and history as examples.

What Is Information Visualization?

In computer science research, the term *visualization* describes the field of study that uses interactive graphical tools to explore and present digitally represented data that might be simulated, measured, or archived.

The visualization field split off from computer graphics in the mid-1980s to distinguish graphics rendered from scientific and engineering data from algorithms for creating images of natural scenes, many of which were a blend of scientific, artistic, and technically pragmatic techniques. A further division occurred in the early 1990s to distinguish scientific, or physically based, data from abstract "information visualization," such as financial data, business records, or collections of documents. More recently, the term *visual analytics* was coined to emphasize the role of analysis, especially for extremely large volumes of data. While these distinctions are valuable as a means of providing different foci for publication, for this discussion they are less important than the commonalities.

The primary publishing venues for research in visualization are the IEEE Visualization Conferences and the supporting IEEE publications, *Transactions on Visualization and Computer Graphics*, and *IEEE Computer Graphics and Applications*. Visualization-relevant work can appear, however, in other fields, including computer graphics, human-computer interaction, vision, perception, and digital design, as well as in fields that extensively use visualization, such as cartography and medicine.

Visualization is not unique to the computer science domain. Edward Tufte has written a series of books on the visualization of information that are considered seminal in the field (Tufte 1990, 1997, 2001). Tufte's books are full of fascinating examples of how information can be graphically presented. Tufte also lectures extensively on the topic, forcefully promoting his personal (usually excellent) views on the best way to present information. Tufte's principles of excellence in visualization emphasize conciseness, clarity, and accuracy.

Graphic designers will assert that the graphical presentation of information is their fundamental goal, which they achieve by applying principles basic to art and design—namely, hierarchies of importance, spatial relationships, layering, contrast versus analogy, legibility, and readability. These elements are constructed from careful choices of positioning, shape, color, size, and typography. Cartographers combine these same elements to create exemplars of information display, as do medical illustrators and other specialists.

Historical Visualization

The following historical examples are often cited in talks and classes on visualization.[1]

William Playfare (1758–1823) is credited as the father of graphical methods in statistics. His inventions include the bar chart, the pie chart, and time-series graphs. His goals were political; his focus was government spending.

John Snow (1813–1858) used a dot plot of cholera cases overlaid on a London street map in 1984 to identify and illustrate the source of the contamination.[2]

Charles Minard (1781–1870) created an information graph published in 1869 illustrating Napoleon's disastrous march to Moscow in the Russian campaign of 1812. The flow diagram, plus its paralleling temperature diagram, poignantly illustrates the number of men that died as the temperature dropped to bitter levels.

The Value of Digital Visualization

Digital visualization enables creation and exploration of large collections of data. I would argue, however, that the tools for collection are far more successful to date than are those for exploration. Other than the ability to explore collections of great size, what value does digital visualization provide?

Digital visualization enables interactive exploration. Compare spreadsheets with graphing capabilities (such as Microsoft's Excel) and dynamic maps (such as Google maps) with their static, paper-based versions. I would argue these two examples are probably the most influential forms of digital information visualization yet discovered.

Digital visualization can be combined with simulation to simultaneously explore many potential solutions along with the probabilities and dependencies that influence them. Brain surgeons, for example, can use the data from a CAT scan to explore different approaches to removing a tumor. Such data can also be used to create simulators for training. Stephen Murray at Columbia has used visualization and simulation in his studies of medieval architecture, such as his digital study of Amiens Cathedral.

Digital visualization can be used to monitor changing streams of data. Many major metropolitan areas have Web sites that show traffic flow in real time, such as the one provided by the Washington State Department of Transportation for the Seattle area.

Digital visualization facilitates collaboration. Collaboration, in the sense of sharing, is fundamental to the Web and to digital archiving. The Web site Many Eyes, however, provides a forum for people to upload their data and create visualizations and for other people to comment on them.

---

1 These three can be found in chapter 1 of Tufte 2001.

2 See Tufte 1997, 27-39 for a complete description.

The Dark Side of Information Visualization

Some are concerned that digital tools are outrunning literacy in the art and science of graphically presenting information. To put it more bluntly, it is too easy to make pictures that confuse, miscommunicate, or downright lie, either inadvertently or deliberately. Tufte's books show many examples of graphical distortion created by inaccurate uses of scale and perspective, extraneous graphical elements ("chart junk"), and improper presentation of data, such as a graph of costs over time that does not adjust the dollar amounts for inflation (Tufte 2001, 53-78).

Even Tufte is not immune to the risk of misusing visualization. After the Challenger disaster, he analyzed and redesigned the graphs used by Morton-Thiokol engineers to communicate their analysis and concluded that if they had visualized their data more effectively, the risk of launching in cold weather would have been clear. This example is frequently used to illustrate the power of visualization (Tufte 1997, 39-50). I recently uncovered a substantial rebuttal by the engineers, which argues that Tufte did not fully understand the context or the data, and is therefore guilty of falsely making the engineers responsible for the disaster (Robison et al. 2002).

A common criticism of visualization tools, both research and commercial, is that they do not embody basic visual design principles. Colors are too bold, lines are too thick, and fonts are too small, these critics claim. The result is cluttered, ugly, and at worst, misleading. The most recent release of Microsoft Office, with its ubiquitous tools Excel and PowerPoint, touts its refined graphics. But the result is a disaster from a visualization standpoint. Colorful, transparent, rotating 3-D bar charts make good "eye candy" but do not communicate their information about their underlying data any more clearly than simple 2-D graphs. In fact, the former are less effective, because the 3-D perspective distorts the numeric relationships represented by the relative heights of the bars.

Stephen Few is a consultant working in the field of business intelligence whose primary mission is to improve the presentation of business graphics. Few's Web site has many examples of terrible visualizations that he has analyzed and redesigned, most made by commercial systems. His book *Show Me the Numbers* teaches how to effectively communicate with simple charts and graphs (Few 2004). This requires understanding the data, the audience, and the problem being solved. These skills must be taught, and I would argue are important for everyone to learn. (Few has an online Graph Design IQ Test to demonstrate this point.)

People's responses to graphics are not purely intellectual; there is a strong visceral and emotional response, as is well appreciated by those in the advertising and entertainment industries. Pictures made from data are no exception, so both authors and consumers need to be educated about the impact of choices in layout, color, typography, and imagery—all topics more commonly taught in courses in art and design.

Creating effective tools for visualization requires technical skills, visualization skills, and a deep understanding of the problems and tasks critical for a particular domain. One common criticism of visualization research is that it presents techniques that are technically interesting but that do not provide solutions to real problems. This is a classic problem in research tool and system design, where technologists have a vision, based on what is computationally possible, but lack an understanding of what is really needed to solve the problems of their potential users. Potential users ("domain experts"), however, can rarely articulate their needs in a way that directly informs the technological development. Successful collaborations that blend the skills of both are all too rare.

Teaching Information Visualization

Information visualization is traditionally taught as a graduate-level course in computer science departments. The focus is on teaching students already fluent in computer systems and technology how to create innovative information visualization tools. Often, the text is Colin Ware's *Information Visualization: Perception for Design* (2004), plus Tufte's *Envisioning Information*, augmented by selected research papers, such as those found in Card et al. (1999). Students in such classes typically create a project, which serves as a basis for their grade in the course.

More recently, courses have been designed to teach information visualization to undergraduates, often those in disciplines other than computer science. With a colleague, Polle Zellweger, I designed and taught an information visualization course as a fourth-year undergraduate elective in the University of Washington iSchool (Info424 2006, 2007). We based our course on other courses, including one taught by Marti Hearst at the University of California, Berkeley (UC Berkeley CS558), and another taught by Melanie Tory at the University of Victoria. We collected material more widely, especially from Pat Hanrahan (Stanford CS448B), John Stasko (Georgia Tech CS7450), and Tamara Munzner (University of British Columbia CPSC 533C). This year, the course is being taught by iSchool doctoral student Marilyn Ostergren, and it includes more visual design plus collaboration with real projects elsewhere on campus (Info424 2008).

We found it an enormous challenge to select the material to be taught. Is the goal to teach students to design visualizations from basic principles or to help them become fluent in existing tools? Should the course focus exclusively on data visualization, or should it include general topics in visual communication? Is the primary goal to make students aware of the broad range of visualization models and tools, or is it to teach them specific skills, such as how to make good data graphs as taught by Few?

Visualization is a skill that must be practiced for fluency, and that takes time. Art and design schools teach visual communication by making students create, critique, and redesign. They assume a fluency in whatever medium is being used. Digital visualization can be taught the same way, but a single class will have to be focused on specific tools and visual forms. Data visualization requires a good understanding of data, how it is structured, basic data manipulation, and statistical analysis. Interactive visualization requires understanding of basic human-computer interaction techniques and the principles that underlie them.

Our choices are reflected in the class Web sites, but I do not believe we have in any way solved this problem, which is a critical one for iSchools. Our efforts to provide concrete skills focused on data graphics, for which we used Stephen Few's book and taught the students how to use the commercial visualization product from Tableau Software. While important, this is too narrow a focus for visualization literacy in iSchools and the humanities. We also used Tufte's *Envisioning Information* for its rich insights, but that does not provide any exposure to interactive and animated visualization. Over two years, we tried several approaches for including interaction principles and skills, relying heavily on examples found on the Web, but were never entirely satisfied.

Color in Visualization and the Visualization of Color

Color is a key element in visualization. It can be used to label, to quantify, to focus attention, and to contribute to the visceral sense of style. The perception and cognition of color is also important and is strongly linked to its usefulness in visualization, as well as to our overall view of nature and the world. The mechanisms for creating color are fascinating and complex, from the displays in nature to the technology of paints, dyes, film, and digital media.

Like visualization, color can be viewed from scientific, artistic, and technical perspectives. Using color effectively requires insight and practice. This section of the paper discusses color literacy as a subspecialty of visualization literacy.

The Craft of Color: An Example

In *Envisioning Information*, Tufte attributes the excellence of Swiss cartography to "good ideas executed with superb craft." The resulting maps pack an immense amount of information into an elegantly useful visual package. Typically, I would now include an image of such a map as an illustration, but it would not capture the beauty of the original, and at worst, would give a completely incorrect impression of its appearance.

Maps are traditionally designed to be printed on paper, with the specific technique depending on the age of the map. I believe the map Tufte admires was designed to be printed on an offset printing press. An offset press prints in inks of different colors, but with no gradation in the color, in contrast to film or displays. For any given spot, ink is either present or not, with high-frequency patterns called "screens" or "halftones" used to vary the lightness. Offset inks may be any of a wide range of colors, and may be transparent or opaque.

The high-quality printed map that Tufte admires would be produced so that each different color was printed as a separate layer, using as many as a dozen printing plates, each with a different color of ink. The design of the map would take every advantage of this process. Each information layer, whether contour lines, grids, text, or the shading to indicate topography, would be crafted to print beautifully.

A commercial offset printer does not have the luxury of unlimited numbers of plates and inks, but instead uses four standard colors: cyan, magenta, yellow, and black. To reproduce a map in a textbook, for example, requires simulating the original map colors by halftoning and combining the standard four colors. Some of the original colors may not be accurately reproducible, which can change the effectiveness of the color encoding. Halftoning also introduces texture. As a result, symbols that were crisp and legible when printed with a solid ink may become fuzzy and less easy to read. A map designed for a commercial offset press, however, would be crafted to ensure that fine lines and text were printed with dark, sufficiently solid colors, and that all colors used in the color encoding would print reliably and distinctly.

Reproducing Tufte's map on a display introduces the complex color-transformation problems between displays and print, and the relative crudeness of the display resolution. Features smaller than a pixel must either become larger or blurred, resulting in illegible or overly bold contour lines, symbols, and text. Maps designed for displays, however, replace these fine features with the ability to dynamically zoom and label. Colors, too, can be dynamic, adding a new dimension to the color encoding.

In all cases, visual perception constrains the choice of line weights, fonts, and colors. The visual factors that affect the legibility of text, symbols, and fine lines are spatial acuity and luminance contrast. *Spatial acuity* is the ability to focus on and discriminate fine patterns of lines (edges); *contrast* is the difference in perceived lightness (luminance) between a foreground object and its background. The choice of colors for rendering and encoding must consider not only luminance contrast but also the effects of simultaneous contrast and spreading.[3]

What can we learn from this example, other than that it is difficult to reproduce color well? First, it should be clear that designing well with color requires knowledge of the materials used to produce it as well as some practical knowledge of human visual perception. It should also be clear that what makes color aesthetic and effective depends on the technical properties of the medium and the culture and economics that support it. Finally, it serves as a warning about the complexity of archiving color: viewing its digital rendering will not be the same as viewing the original object.

---

3 For more information on color perception, technology, and the difficulties of transferring colors across media, see Stone 2003.

Color Design Guidelines: Do No Harm

Tufte's primary rule for color design is "Do no harm." The complete quote talks both of the power of color in visualization and its ability to confuse, and therefore recommends using color sparingly and only for very specific purposes that he calls "fundamental uses." These uses are "*to label* (color as noun), *to measure* (color as quantity), *to represent or imitate reality* (color as representation), and *to enliven or decorate* (color as beauty)" (Tufte 1990, 81). Consider this map of the area around the Point Reyes National Seashore, designed by the National Park Service. Color is used extensively to label, including the roads (whose different shades of red indicate their relative size), the cities, the land, the water, and the park area.[4] Using blue for water and green for the park is an example of imitating reality, which is typically done in an illustrative rather than a realistic way. The map is designed to read well when reproduced in shades of gray, but the color version is both more aesthetic and effective.

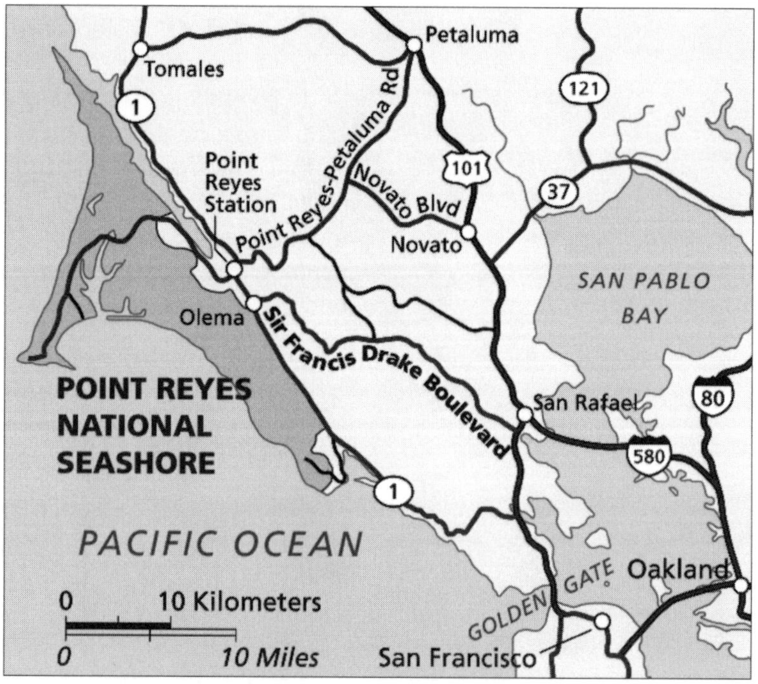

Fig. 1: Region map for Point Reyes.
Courtesy of the US National Park Service.

The following map, taken from the Census Atlas of the United States, uses color to indicate population density. The darker the color, the higher the density, as indicated in the legend. This is an example of color as quantity. This type of color encoding is used extensively in data maps like this one (called a chloropleth map), and also in more abstract information visualizations, such as the color-coded "Map of the Market" presented on the SmartMoney.com Web site.

---

[4] Please see the online version of this publication for color renditions of Figures 1 and 2, available at http://www.clir.org/pubs/abstract/pub145abst.html.

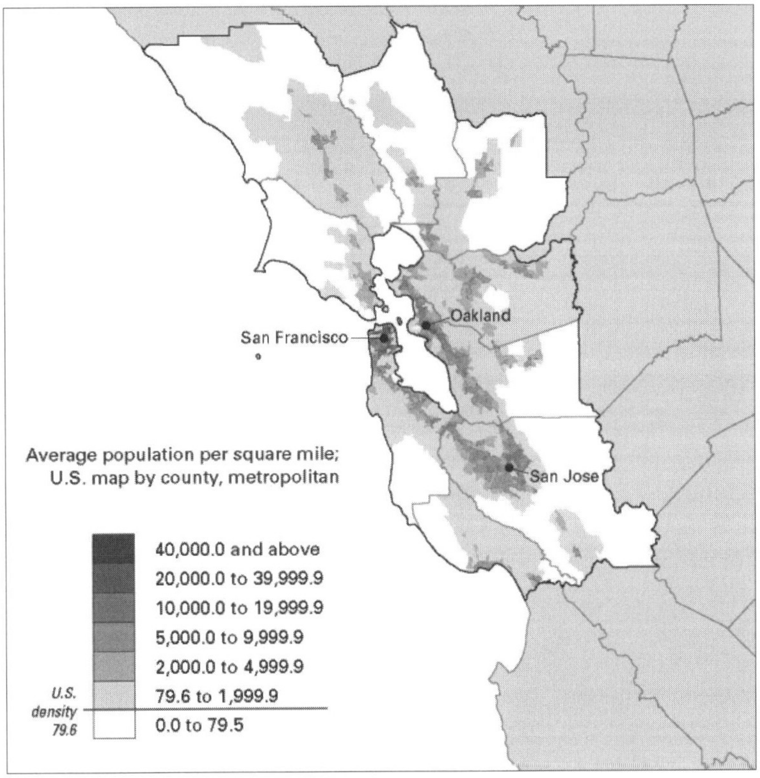

Fig. 2: Population density for the San Francisco Bay area. Courtesy of the U.S. Census Bureau.

Learning how to do excellent visual design takes dedication, skill, and practice. With appropriate tools and guidelines, learning to avoid making awful visualizations may be simpler.

Example: Voting System Guidelines

Under contract with the National Institute of Standards and Technology (NIST), I recently wrote a set of guidelines for the use of color in voting systems (Stone et al. 2008). A primary motivation was to ensure accessibility for individuals with color vision deficiencies, but we were able to create guidelines that should greatly improve the use of color for everyone. The irony is that color use in paper ballots is usually constrained by the economics of printing—white paper, black text, perhaps one other color for labeling. But, given a color digital display in a voting kiosk, developers now have the opportunity to use, and to grossly misuse, color.

Our objective was to create a simple, testable set of rules that would eliminate the gross misuses of color and encourage its proper use. Our first goal was legibility, which is most easily achieved by severely restricting the use of colored text. Our second goal was to avoid the "color chaos" caused by the indiscriminate use of color. For this we required a consistent mapping between color and its function.

Example: Make the Easy Choice the Right One

Tools for creating visualizations have the opportunity to encode good practice in their design. An example is the system created by Tableau Software for data exploration and visualization. Tableau Software is the outgrowth of research at Stanford University on data visualization and analysis. It is run on a workstation that makes it easy to interactively create charts, graphs, and data maps to explore a database of numerical and categorical information. Fundamental to the design of the user interface for this system is the desire to make it easy for the user to create effective, aesthetic visualizations.

I worked with Tableau to design the colors and, equally important, the interfaces used for assigning colors to their data visualizations, which consist of tables, graphs, scatter plots, and bar charts. As well as designing color palettes that were legible and uniquely colored (for labels), or smoothly varying (for quantity), I worked with the developers to design user interfaces that encouraged good use of color.

Most color-selection tools allow users to choose a color point in some color space. The guiding principle for the Tableau user interface, by contrast, is to map a set of colors to data. For labeling, users first select a palette, or set of coordinated colors, that can be applied in one operation to the entire data set. Users can also select individual colors from different palettes, or even customize individual colors using a traditional color tool, but the simplest operation is to accept the default palette, or to choose a similarly well-crafted one. A similar approach was used for the colored ramps used to map colors to data.

My colleagues at Simon Fraser University and I have begun some studies of grids and other visual reference structures that are traditionally designed to be low contrast, yet legible (Bartram and Stone 2007; Stone et al. 2006). Graphic designers can layer information without causing visual clutter by controlling the relative contrast of the data elements. The elements can be designed for a specific set of information and medium, but in digital visualization, both are dynamic. We seek ways to understand and quantify the subtle aspects of visual representation required in dense information displays so that they can be algorithmically manipulated to match human requirements in interactive and dynamic conditions.

Our approach to this problem is not to characterize "ideal" or "best" but to define boundary conditions outside of which the presentation is clearly bad. We reason that the best solution will always depend on context as well as on individual taste. Boundary conditions are likely to have simple rules that can easily be incorporated by engineers and researchers and are less likely to be influenced by individual taste.

Visualizing Color

That colors change when reproduced is not new with digital media. Posters of great artworks provide only an impression of the original work. Nonetheless, such reproductions have value. The important thing is to understand their context and limitations, and then to augment them with additional analysis and information. Even a crude reproduction can answer basic questions about form, layout, and even color and shading. The change in painting style from medieval images of the Madonna (which are flat and feature a wealth of gold leaf), to the paintings of Rubens, with their lush and subtle shading, should be clear in even the most basic of reproductions. A comparison in any depth of thirteenth-century colors with those of Rubens, however, should be approached cautiously and should not depend on pictorial reproductions alone.

In *The Bright Earth*, Philip Ball (2003) persuasively argues that to fully appreciate color in art requires an understanding of both the chemistry and economics of color: the Virgin's blue cloak colored with pigment made from ground lapis lazuli is not only beautiful but expensive, reflecting the status of the patron who commissioned it. In a digital visualization, we may not see the proper colors, but we could link to discussions of historical color, to a spectral analysis of the particular paint, and to a symbolic visualization of the color relationships in the painting.

Art curators and historians know that colors change over time, so that the colors of an "original" as seen today are not the same as they were when the work was new. A dramatic example is the discovery that Greek and Roman statues, whose white purity had been held as an artistic ideal for generations, were originally painted. These theories are supported by surface analysis of the stone as well as by historical references to painted, lifelike statues (Gurewitsch 2008).

To illustrate the effect of the coloring, full-size models have been created and colored with historically accurate paints. Pictures of these reproductions, with their shockingly bright colors, are effective illustrations. Viewing the models themselves, however, will provide a much more accurate impression than any picture, just as viewing Michelangelo's towering statue of David is very different from looking at a picture of it. This is not just a limitation of imaging; it is a fundamental part of perception.

The digital data used to create the models could be used to create a virtual model in 3-D, which could then be dynamically colored to explore competing theories of coloring. It seems likely, for example, that the bold colors proposed so far are merely the undercoat of a subtler coloring, and would have been refined with layers of sophisticated overpainting. Three-dimensional graphics models of antiquities are now routinely used to illustrate and explore archaeological data (e.g., Pieta [Bernardini et al. 2002], Digital Michelangelo [Levoy et al. 2000]). Differences in pigments, lighting, and painting styles could all be explored and compared.

A good example of digital color reconstruction is the work done on rejuvenating the palette for Seurat's *Sunday on La Grande Jatte,* which hangs in the Art Institute in Chicago. The colors of the original painting, especially those containing zinc yellow, have darkened and yellowed over time. By simulating the physical properties of this pigment and translating them to color, Roy Berns and his colleagues have been able to simulate the original appearance of the painting (Berns n.d.).

Summary: Be Literate about Data, Skeptical about Pictures

In summary, the effective distillation of knowledge from information requires tools, one class of which is the abstracted graphical presentations called information visualizations. Digital information visualization provides potentially tremendous power, but also risk. Its effective design and use, like that of all powerful tools, requires education, training, and iterative refinement.

The hypermedia and computational underpinnings of Web 2.0 provide more-than-adequate technology. What is needed are insight and good design to apply this power to studies in the humanities. Most critical is active involvement by those most interested in the results. Their information goals must drive the tools, not the inverse.

Literacy in information analysis requires a willingness to grapple with data in all its untidy forms, including missing, incomplete, and contradictory entries. Good scholarship involves moving through layers of abstraction, using visualization to summarize, and drilling down to the supporting information structures. Good tools for scholarship must always include ways to view the underlying assumptions, to visualize and examine alternative interpretations, and to expose the degree of uncertainty.

The pictures generated as information visualization must be crafted with care and viewed with suspicion. Then they will correctly have the ability "to express 10,000 words."[5]

References

Ball, Phillip. 2003. *Bright Earth: Art and the Invention of Color*. Chicago: University of Chicago Press.

Bartram, Lyn, and Maureen Stone. Don't Scream: Characterizing Subtle Grids. Poster presentation at IEEE Visualization 2007, Oct. 28-Nov. 1, 2007, Sacramento, Calif.

[5] With due respect to Larkin and Simon (1987).

Bernardini, F., H. Rushmeier, I. M. Martin, J. Mittleman, and G. Taubin. 2002. Building a Digital Model of Michelangelo's Florentine Pieta. *IEEE Computer Graphics and Applications* 22(1): 59-67.

Berns, Roy S. n.d. *Rejuvenating Seurat's Palette Using Color and Imaging Science: A Simulation*. Available at http://www.cis.rit.edu/people/faculty/berns/seurat/Seurat_Berns_Essay_small.pdf

Card, Stuart, Jock Mackinaly, Ben Shneiderman. 1999. *Readings in Information Visualization: Using Vision to Think*. San Francisco: Morgan Kaufman.

Few, Stephen. 2004. *Show Me the Numbers*. Oakland, Calif.: Analytics Press.

Gurewitsch, Matthew. 2008. True Colors. *Smithsonian* magazine (July).

Larkin, Jill H. and Herbert A. Simon. 1987. Why a Diagram is (Sometimes) Worth Ten Thousand Words. *Cognitive Science* 11(1): 65-100.

Levoy, M., K. Pulli, B. Curless, S. Rusinkiewicz, D. Koller, L. Pereira, M. Ginzton, S. Anderson, J. Davis, J. Ginsberg, J. Shade, and D. Fulk. 2000. The Digital Michelangelo Project: 3D Scanning of Large Statues. In *Proceedings of the 27th Annual Conference on Computer Graphics and Interactive Technique*, 131-144. New York: ACM Press/Addison-Wesley Publishing Co., New York, NY, 131-144.

Robison, Wade, Roger Boisjoly, David Hoeker, and Stefan Young. 2002. Representation and Misrepresentation: Tufte and the Morton Thiokol Engineers on the Challenger. *Science and Engineering Ethics* 8(1): 59-81. Guildford, Surrey, UK: Opragen Publications. Available at http://www.onlineethics.org/cms/17453.aspx.

Stone, Maureen, Sharon J. Laskowsi, and Svetlana Z. Lowry. 2008. *Guidelines for Using Color in Voting Systems*. National Institute of Standards and Technology (NISTIR 7537). Available at http://vote.nist.gov/NISTIR-7537.pdf

Stone, Maureen, Lyn Bartram, and Diane Gromala. 2006. Great Grids: How and Why? In *ACM SIGGRAPH 2006 Research Posters*. International Conference on Computer Graphics and Interactive Techniques, July 30-Aug. 3, 2006, Boston, Mass. New York: ACM.

Stone, Maureen. 2003. *A Field Guide to Digital Color*. Wellesley, Mass.: A. K. Peters.

Tufte, Edward R. 2001 (1983). *The Visual Display of Quantitative Information*, second ed. Cheshire, Conn.: Graphics Press.

Tufte, Edward R. 1997. *Visual Explanations*. Cheshire Conn.: Graphics Press.

Tufte, Edward R. 1990. *Envisioning Information*. Cheshire Conn.: Graphics Press.

Ware, Colin. 2004. *Information Visualization: Perception for Design*, 2nd ed. San Francisco: Morgan Kaufman.

Web sites

Amiens Cathedral Web site: http://www.learn.columbia.edu/Mcahweb/Amiens.html.

Google maps: http://maps.google.com/.

IEEE Visualization Conferences: http://vis.computer.org/.

Many Eyes: http://manyeyes.alphaworks.ibm.com.

SmartMoney: http://smartmoney.com.

Stephen Few's Web site: http://www.perceptualedge.com/.

Tableau Software: http://www.tableausoftware.com/.

University of Washington iSchool: http://www.ischool.washington.edu/. The URL for the current course is:
http://courses.washington.edu/info424/ (this is the 2008 course).
The courses Zellweger and Stone taught are archived at:
http://courses.washington.edu/info424/2006/
http://courses.washington.edu/info424/2007/

U.S. Census Atlas: http://www.census.gov/population/www/cen2000/censusatlas/.

Washington State Department of Transportation: http://www.wsdot.wa.gov/Traffic/seattle/.

Art History and the New Media: Representation and the Production of Humanistic Knowledge

Stephen Murray

Since the reflections that follow will unavoidably respond to my own peculiar experiences and interests, it may be helpful to start with a quick sketch of where I came from. Educated as a historian, first of medieval economic history and then of medieval architectural production, I am interested primarily in issues of representation. In my search to represent a past that has vanished—like the snows of last winter—the relative permanence of stone buildings has an obvious appeal, while at the same time presenting a most intriguing and engaging range of problems of response and representation.

As an art historian (at Indiana, Harvard, and Columbia Universities), I have been committed to the propagation of my own field of study (medieval art); to the institutional well-being of my academic departments (two of which I chaired); and to the advancement of my discipline through teaching. I have sponsored about 40 doctoral dissertations in as many years and have taught some 25 summer programs introducing young scholars and others to the monuments of medieval architecture. I played a leading role in the introduction of the new media into art historical teaching and research in the mid-1990s.

At what point did I become aware of the power of the media to transform the way we do business? My formative experience came some 40 years ago when, with a group of fellow Oxford undergraduates, I set out to make a documentary film on Armenian church architecture for the BBC program *Travellers' Tales*. Entirely without film experience, we drove across Asia Minor to Armenia equipped with a Bell & Howell movie camera that we wound up, set upon a flimsy tripod, and pointed at Ani Cathedral. The camera clicked and whirred, but our expectations that the monument would somehow *do* something were, of course, unfulfilled: we could have achieved exactly the same results with a still photograph. This was the start of a powerful interest in the spatial animation of works of architecture that culminated in my 1994 Amiens Cathedral Project and my establishment of the Media Center for Art History at Columbia University under a National Endowment for the Humanities Challenge Grant.

I have chosen here to focus on the application of the new media in relation to two aspects of art history—representation and the production of knowledge. Let me begin with some reflections on the first issue.

Representation

Art history is about representation. It begins when an interlocutor stands in front of a work of art and talks. In the classroom, however, we make a virtue out of dealing with the absence of the work of art, which is represented by a surrogate image. For more than 100 years, this surrogate most frequently came in the form of juxtaposed images created with slides. Standing in front of two such images, the teacher might announce to the class, "The slide on the right is Autun Cathedral; the slide on the left is Chartres." Each monument is then analyzed in terms of its essential characteristics; similarities and differences are distinguished, and the question is raised as to how, in the course of the twelfth century, we get from Autun to Chartres. In this way, the teacher's rhetoric has tended to privilege temporal developments (from Romanesque to Gothic), and students are encouraged to believe in a story of progress from "early" to "high" and "late" manifestations. This kind of story, or entelechy—one in which the outcome is known at the start—is inherently boring. Most troublesome, however, is the notion that a single two-dimensional image could possibly "be" Chartres Cathedral, which is, of course, a space-enclosing monument, rooted in the French landscape at least 3,000 miles away from most U.S. students.

In the second half of the twentieth century, scholars of all kinds for all kinds of reasons began to reject the old art historical rhetoric with its endless accounts of stylistic "developments" and "influences." Their discipline was animated through the infusion of notions derived mainly from social and anthropological studies, as well as from literary criticism. This first revolution, the "literary turn" of the 1960s–1980s, was followed in the 1990s by a second revolution—the new availability of an astonishing range of media made possible by the miniaturization of video hardware, digital technology, new editing and animation software, and, finally, the Internet. Oddly, however, the attitudes of many art historians toward image technology remained extremely conservative; struggles developed between those who remained committed to the intense study of the works of art themselves and those who preferred to philosophize about the discipline at a safe distance from the works of art. Those who were the most radical in their desire to transform the intellectual underpinnings of art history were sometimes the most reactionary as far as changes in image technology were concerned.

My own engagement with the media was rekindled at this time through the opportunity to make a short film on Beauvais Cathedral in association with Greenberg Associates. The film was part of the program of Art on Film launched in the late 1980s by the J. Paul Getty Foundation with the Metropolitan Museum of Art. The production team animated the forms and spaces of the cathedral by abandoning the fixed tripod and mounting the camera on a dolly moving on rails, on a crane, and on a helicopter. Participation in that effort enabled me to redeem the frustration of the earlier project to film Ani Cathedral.

We had no difficulty in allowing Saint-Pierre of Beauvais to star in his own movie, but a new question then arose: What do we listen to as we move through and around the stunningly beautiful spaces of Beauvais Cathedral, animated through the passage of the camera? The new media will allow us to create a simulacrum of the spatial envelope of the cathedral that is much closer to the original work than any slide. Given the immediacy of the images that we can now create, do we still need to hear the voice of the interlocutor with his or her interminable rhetoric? Fear of the power of a lifelike simulacrum may actually have lain behind some of the initial opposition to the new media. But the cathedral was itself created as a medium—a means of getting you from one place to another—and the words of the interlocutor might actually hinder that passage.

An animation of a work of art through film, video, or virtual reality can be a powerful tool for teachers, allowing them to bring the work into their classrooms with a new kind of force. The absence of a voice-over commentary can allow teachers to experiment with multiple viewpoints. Such an approach, employed in the Amiens Project (1994) undertaken by the Media Center for Art History to serve the Columbia Core Curriculum, certainly changed the means of representation available to the teacher wanting to bring a surrogate image into the classroom.

Production of Knowledge

But what about the other task identified in the title of my paper—the production of knowledge? Knowledge may, of course, be created though the systematic looking demanded by the business of representation as the inherent qualities of the work of art are elucidated through verbal description. But as the interlocutor describes the work of art, he or she will invoke not only what members of the audience can see but also what they cannot see. Thus, the affirmation "This is a Gothic cathedral" makes sense only when we relate the work of architecture before our eyes to a thousand other such buildings. In the controlled space of the classroom, the teacher contrives juxtaposed images to tell a story. It is the same with a picture: the forms and events depicted, and even the manner of depiction, take on levels of meaning when related to what is "out there," beyond the frame of the picture.

But a problem arises when we attempt to fix the meaning of the work of art in relation to the "out there." At the moment when a work of art is created, a thousand different possibilities and relationships exist; at the moment of representation, however, this range may be compressed into a single path fixed on the pages of a book or into the essentially linear pattern of classroom rhetoric. The notion of context is particularly troublesome, since students will inevitably construct different contexts to accommodate their own preconceptions and prejudices.

Contextualization, then, demands a spatial, rather than a linear, environment. This is particularly true for architecture, which is itself a space-enclosing entity rooted in the space of the landscape. Henri Lefebvre (*La Production de l'espace*, 1974) has invited us to consider the dynamism of linkages between a range of different kinds of space: mnemonic, social, geopolitical, urban, architectural. Such thoughts are particularly relevant to the understanding of Romanesque and Gothic architecture—a phenomenon involving the production of hundreds of edifices in a context of dynamic interactions among clergy, nobility, and newly wealthy townsfolk within a cultural context of rapidly emerging national identity. To what extent did the architecture of Romanesque and Gothic result from such identities, or to what extent did it create those identities? More specifically, what was the role of Gothic architecture in the creation of France? It is difficult to answer such questions and to fix such relationships within a unified story on the pages of a book. A computer provides a better environment for the exploration of such problems.

Let me illustrate this concept with reference to "Mapping Gothic France," a databasing project on Gothic architecture that I am currently undertaking with support from The Andrew W. Mellon Foundation.[1] The idea of databasing Gothic architecture, rather than stringing the monuments along in a linear sequence or "story," is not new: it belongs to the venerable intellectual tradition of the *statistique monumental*, a phenomenon growing out of the encyclopedic movement of the eighteenth century. Many volumes have been published as alphabetically arranged catalogs of monuments from particular regions of France or other European countries. We might also remember the ostensive formlessness of Viollet-le-Duc's alphabetically arranged *Dictionnaire raisonné de l'architecture française* of the 1850s.

What the computer can do is to arrange a collection of monuments in the spatial environment of a map, rather than in a linear or an alphabetical sequence on the pages of a book. The space between buildings is just as important as the space inside them. Each monument should be presented with plans and sections rendered on the same scale and with some indication of raw dimensions. It should be possible to visit each monument with high-resolution photographs presented not as "thumbnails" on a "page" but in meaningful relationship to the experience of the visit—reflecting the approach to and

[1] The project is a collaborative one: my coprincipal investigator is Andrew Tallon, professor of art history at Vassar College. During the summer we traveled together to gather the data for the Web site, we were accompanied by two Vassar and two Columbia students. We also worked closely with Professor Arnaud Timbert of Lille University and some of his doctoral students.

entrance into the monument and passage through and around its spaces. The spatial integrity of the building is represented through panoramic images (QTVR) and three-dimensional models.

Such a program offers extraordinary potential in the generation of knowledge, in its application in the classroom, and in the fostering of new kinds of collaborative networks.

The new kind of knowledge may perhaps be best understood in relation to "The Garden of Forking Paths," a short story by Jorge Victor Borges. In this story, Borges addresses the impossibility of writing a conventional book representing all the potential outcomes of all the bifurcations faced in the garden of life. In building a great medieval church, the builders certainly must have reached some kind of consensus prior to the start of work. In the half-century or more during which construction took place, however, multiple opportunities for change undoubtedly arose. The initial choices must have soon seemed old-fashioned or structurally inappropriate given the dynamic behavior of arched masonry. A procession of visiting critical experts would express their reservations about the work, attempting in this way to impose their own services ("it's too dark; your capital sculpture is outdated; the flying buttresses are too high to be effective; it's going to fall down," etc.) The building accounts of Troyes Cathedral document exactly such a continuing situation.

Each cathedral construction project must, then, be understood as a kind of continuing event, embodying all the decisions made over the decades or centuries of construction. A military engagement such as the Battle of Bouvines (1214) may unfold in a single day and may imprint its outcome definitively upon history. A cathedral also continues to impose its presence, but its forms must be understood as the result of multiple choices made by human agents with different agendas in circumstances that might be quite volatile. It is not enough for teachers to tell their students of this situation: the possibility of visiting hundreds of buildings located on the map will allow them to make this discovery for themselves. We hope, moreover, to provide animated maps that will take the student back to the dangerous middle decades of the twelfth century, when the future shape of the nations of western Europe was far from clear, with confrontations between Capetian and Plantagenet, Christianity and Islam, North and South, Catholic and "heretic." The laying out on the ground of hundreds of related buildings in this period of uncertainty was certainly a means of fixing the desired outcome.

I want to close with a reflection on the linkage between the agency of a group of people who conspire to fix a desired future in a time of uncertainty and the activity of a group of builders who lay out a great church on the ground within a space marked out by stretched ropes. Both activities may be understood as plotting. The cathedral plot, then, includes not only physical control of the terrain vague of the intended building site but also the establishment in human terms of shared desire and the logistical means to accomplish the project. My own desire, finally, is to provide an environment in which students can rediscover the astonishing implications of the plotting of Gothic France.

Social Attention in the Age of the Web

Bernardo A. Huberman

The Internet is slowly but irreversibly changing ideas we've had for centuries about libraries as unique repositories of knowledge. What started as a digital medium for transmitting data and computer programs soon morphed into the World Wide Web, which in about a decade transformed forever the way people think of information and the ways in which they access it. We no longer need to physically enter a library to obtain the latest news or to read a scholarly journal. A simple search through any computer or mobile device having a browser and a keyboard is enough to put at our disposal not only what we search for but also a trove of related findings that increase our curiosity and expand our horizons. Add to that the ubiquity of e-mail and instant messaging, and we find ourselves in a world of instant connectivity and potentially productive connections with social networks across the globe.

What are we to make of such a world? To start with, instant and free access to information across geographic and institutional boundaries has made its value plummet in an economic sense. We value what is scarce, not what is plentiful, and the precious entity is now *attention*, which is always finite and claimed by many sources at the same time. The Web has made possible the creation and display of content that, it is hoped, multitudes will attend to. Thus the keen competition for people's attention, manifested through e-mails, blogs, and manuscripts that keep appearing on our screens.

The kind of attention that I have in mind is social in nature, and while recognizing that the perceptual component of individual attention is central to the whole process, I will focus on the intensity (i.e., the number of visits, links, and citations) of signals pointing to a given idea, result, paper, Web site, etc. This in turn brings into focus the role that social networks of all kinds play in the amount of attention allocated to topics of interest to a discussion group.

Attention is so important in the world of academia[1] that I'd venture to state that it is often its main currency: we publish to get the attention of others, we cite so that other researchers' work gets attention, and we cherish the prominence of great work if only because of the attention it gathers. This phenomenon has been taking place since the establishment of learned societies and academic disciplines, but it has not been analyzed systematically until recently. Recent work (Goldhaber 1998; Franck 1999; Klamer and Van Dalen 2002; Falkinger 2007; Huberman and Wu 2008; Wu and Huberman 2007) is starting to frame this problem in the context of the new digital medium while providing insights on the role that attention plays both in the Web and in electronic publishing. Richard Lanham (2006) has eloquently described the significant role that the arts and letters play in this attention economy by creating attention structures that often trump style over content.

A recent study we performed at HP Labs provides a stark example of how attention drives content creation outside the academy or enterprise (Huberman, Romero, and Wu 2008). Analysis of a massive YouTube data set revealed that the productivity of those uploading videos strongly depends on attention, as measured by the number of downloads. Conversely, a lack of attention leads to a decrease in the number of videos uploaded and a consequent drop in productivity, which in many cases asymptotes to no uploads whatsoever. Most of the YouTube content shares this fate, as the consumption of uploaded content is highly skewed. Whereas most videos are never downloaded, a few get a disproportionate share of the audience's attention.

This result offers insight into how the tragedy of the digital commons is partially averted. Basically, contributors treat the digital commons as a private good, in which payment for their efforts is in the form of the attention that their content gathers. The result is a massive contribution to the public good.

The relevant question is how attention allocation, and its impact on research, is transformed by the advent of digital media and the consequent flood of information that streams into our senses, as well as by the new modalities exemplified by Wikipedia and Web-based social networks that span the globe.

For academics, the panacea offered by the Web is tempered by the fact that even the best Web sites are at times insufficient to provide the information they seek while filtering out unnecessary content. While some sites decide what to display on the basis of an objective criterion (e.g., novelty of a paper or image, page rank in search, popularity of a topic, or the salience of news), they do not necessarily maximize the user's value. For example, an algorithm such as Google's page rank inserts the most linked-to pages in the first page of a query result, but other links in other pages often con-

[1] That attention is a valued resource in general, and that people are willing to forsake financial gain to obtain it has been empirically demonstrated by B. A. Huberman, C. Loch, and A. Onculer. 2004. Status as a Valued Resource. *Social Psychology Quarterly* 67(1): 103–114.

tain incipiently valuable information that is not available to the user just because they are buried further down the list.

Another problem stems from the finite number of items that a user can attend to in a given time interval. This psychological constraint is compounded by a strong empirical regularity observed in Web browsing that goes under the name of "the law of surfing" (Huberman et al. 1998; Huberman 2002). This law states that the probability of a user accessing a number of Web pages in a single session markedly decays with the number of pages, thereby constraining the amount of information that ever gets explored in a single surfing session. A typical user seldom visits pages beyond the first one displaying search results; consequently, a page ranked near the bottom by a search engine is unlikely to be viewed by many users. This behavior tends to reinforce the leading position of those top items and to further increase their popularity, which in turn penalizes content that is not yet well known. Thus, it is easy for an item to get locked in a top ranking and hard for other bottom items to surface, even though the latter can often be more valuable.

In spite of all these obstacles, we somehow manage to remain up-to-date with our work; once in a while, we even discover interesting facts and ideas that are relevant to our intellectual endeavors. We often accomplish this through a social network of like-minded academics, colleagues, and friends who quickly propagate novel ideas and their opinions about them. These networks, sometimes called "informal colleges" or "communities of practice," were identified a long time ago as important channels for the dissemination and validation of new results in a given discipline (Crane 1972; Crozier 1964). The advent of the Web has increased the scope and swiftness of these networks by several orders of magnitude.

Social networks are not restricted to academia. Any infrastructure that provides opportunities for communication among its members is eventually threaded by communities of people who have similar goals and a shared understanding of their activities. These informal networks coexist with the formal structure of any organization and serve many purposes, such as deciding on the relative worth of given results (and at times the reputations of the authors of these results), solving problems more efficiently (Feld 1981), and furthering the interests of their members. Despite their lack of official recognition, informal networks can provide effective ways of learning and actually enhance the productivity of the formal organization.

In the digital domain, we are witnessing a proliferation of social networks, such as Facebook, Myspace, Linkedin, and Hnet, that connect very large and geographically extended social groups while providing them with a sense of immediacy that fosters the exchange of information on myriad topics and types of media.

This new social trend has sparked a keen interest in identifying online communities. Some of this work finds that online relationships do indeed reflect actual social relationships, thus adding to the "social capital" of a community. Mailing lists and personal Web pages also serve as proxies for social relationships, and the communities identified from these online proxies resemble the actual social communities of the represented individuals.

Research on the role of social networks in the dissemination of ideas, purchases, and reputations is also accelerating because of the ease with which data can be gathered and analyzed on a scale that was impossible using traditional methods (Wasserman and Faust 1994). As an example, the figure below displays the results of an analysis of a network of recommendations responsible for the purchase of books. The study focused on data from Amazon, containing 15 million recommendations of books recommended to more than 5 million people who purchased them (Leskovek, Adamic, and Huberman 2007). By studying the networks that grew up around each book—who bought and recommended it, and who responded to the recommendation—we learned that social networks take on different characteristics depending on the type of books that were recommended. In the figure, red dots and lines indicate people who purchased a product while blue dots and lines represent people who received a recommendation.[2] The network around a medical book (small graph in the upper left-hand corner) shows a scattered network where recommendations, on average, don't travel very far. On the other hand, the network surrounding a Japanese graphic novel, which occupies the central part of the picture, shows a thick flow of information among densely connected groups of people.

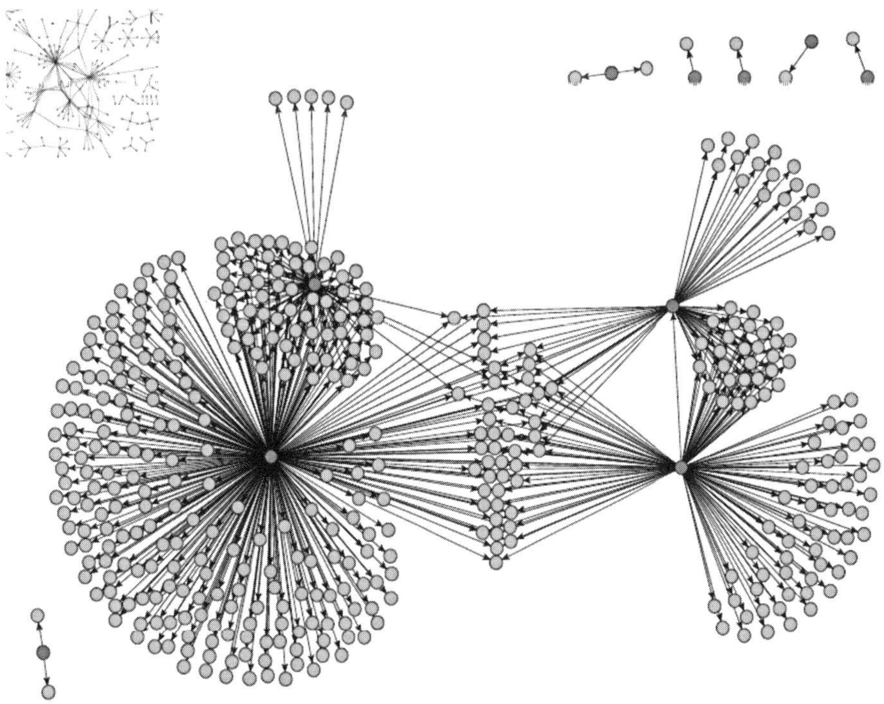

[2] Please see the online version of this publication for a color rendition of this figure above, available at http://www.clir.org/pubs/abstract/pub145abst.html.

The same methodology used to discover the social network underlying the propagation of recommendations may be used for any other kind of information linking people. For example, several years ago we developed a fully automated method for identifying communities of practice within an organization by studying the patterns of e-mail exchanges among its members (Tyler, Wilkinson, and Huberman 2003; Huberman and Adamic 2004). The method uses e-mail data to construct a network of correspondences, and then discovers the communities by partitioning this network in a particular way, as described below. The only pieces of information used from each e-mail were the names of the sender and receiver (i.e., the "To:" and "From:" fields), enabling the processing of a large number of e-mails while minimizing privacy concerns.

Using this method and a standard desktop PC, we were able to identify small communities within a globally distributed organization in a matter of hours. Interviews validated the results obtained by our automated process and provided interesting perspectives on the communities identified. Other approaches have used coauthorship of papers to identify social networks (Kempe, Kleinberg, and Tardos 2003), which can also be useful if one is interested in tracking the evolution of cooperation within disciplines. And since social structure affects the flow of information, knowledge of the communities that exist within a network can also be used for navigating the networks when searching for individuals or resources (Huberman and Adamic 2004; Kempe, Kleinberg, and Tardos 2003).

An important aspect of social networks is how they direct attention to given topics or results while ignoring others. Collective attention is at the heart of the spread of ideas and the reputations of people, and it has been studied at the individual and small-group levels by a number of psychologists, economists, and researchers in the area of marketing and advertising. Attention also affects the propagation of information in social networks, determining the effectiveness of advertising and viral marketing. While progress on this problem has been made in small laboratory studies and in the theoretical literature of attention economics, it is only recently that we have obtained empirical results from very large groups in a natural, nonlaboratory setting (Wu and Huberman 2007).

To understand how social networks mediate the allocation of attention, consider how a news story spreads. When it first comes out, the story catches the attention of a few, who may pass it on to others in their social network if they find it interesting enough. If a lot of people start to pay attention to this story, its exposure in the media will continue to increase. In other words, a positive reinforcement effect sets in: the more popular the story becomes, the faster it spreads. This growth is counterbalanced by the fact that the novelty of a story tends to fade with time and that people therefore pay less attention to it.

Thus, with respect to the dynamics of collective attention, two competing effects are present: (1) the growth in the number of people that attend to a given story; and (2) the habituation that makes the same story less likely to be attractive as time goes on. This process becomes more complex when multiple items or stories appear at the same time and people must decide which stories to attend to. However simplistic this description might be, it allows for the construction of a mathematical model that predicts how attention is allocated among many items, links, and other factors, and how those items become less novel over time (Wu and Huberman 2007).

The predictions of this theory, which were empirically tested with a million users of a popular news site (digg.com) are as follows: (1) the distribution of attention among a set of items is log-normally distributed, i.e., it is highly skewed in such a way that most stories get a typical small number of "diggs" (as a measure of the attention they receive), whereas a few receive a lot of attention (a winner-take-all scenario); and (2) collective attention decays slowly, specifically in the form of a stretched exponential function of time.

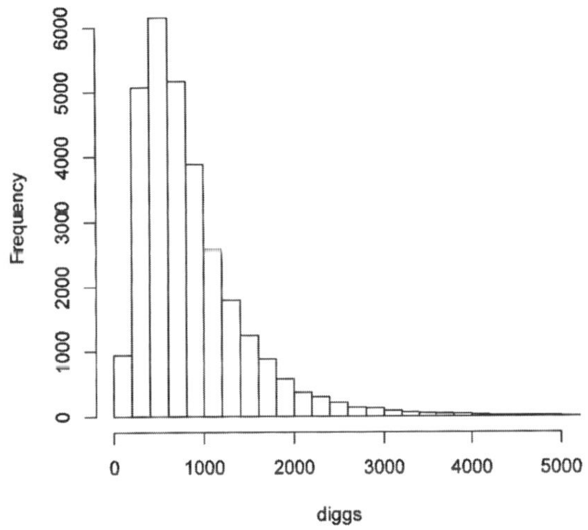

The figure above, which shows the distribution of attention over all stories in digg.com, clearly displays the skewed behavior just described. This distribution, with its long tail, provides another plausible explanation to the question of why the large majority of articles in the sciences receive so little attention whereas a small percentage (i.e., those in the tail of the distribution) make the grade in terms of a large number of citations.

But this is still not the complete story. Other drivers can be as effective as novelty in eliciting social attention. One is popularity, which often leads us to read and examine ideas if only because others do. Another is style, as is the case when visual elements make an idea or presentation initially compelling because of its elegance or esthetic value. Much research is needed to elucidate all these aspects, and we are currently examining some others as well, such as the role of attention in opinion formation on the Web and its role in the productivity of individuals.

In conclusion, I hope to have shown that in the age of the Web, social attention and its swift allocation through vast social networks plays a central role in the dissemination and validation of ideas and results within the academic community. Two very successful examples bracket my statement. Wikipedia has already shown the power of an interactive medium in creating a vast landscape of knowledge, even when the threshold for contributions is negligible and authorship remains anonymous. At the other extreme, many practitioners of a highly technical branch of the hard sciences, superstring theory in particle physics, have opted out of the traditional publication venues and chosen to exchange their manuscripts through an electronic preprint repository (arxiv.org) without going through standard refereeing procedures. In both cases, the intense chatter of these worldwide communities brings attention to relevant results and serves as a good quality filter.

And given that this essay is about attention and that I'm keenly aware of its fleeting nature, I think that it would be unwise to continue writing beyond this point.

References

Crane, D. 1972. *Invisible Colleges: Diffusion of Knowledge in Scientific Communities*. Chicago: University of Chicago Press.

Crozier, M. 1964. *The Bureaucratic Phenomenon*. Chicago: University of Chicago Press.

Falkinger, J. 2007. Attention Economies. *Journal of Economic Theory* 133: 266–294.

Feld, S. L. 1981. The Focused Organization of Social Ties. *American Journal of Sociology* 86: 1015-1035.

Franck G. 1999. Science Communication, a Vanity Fair. *Science* 286: 53–55.

Goldhaber, M. H. 1998. Attention Economics and the Net. *First Monday* 2.

Huberman, B. A. and F. Wu. 2008. The Economics of Attention: Maximizing User Value in Information-Rich Environments. *Advances in Complex Systems* 11(4): 487-496.

Huberman, B. A., D. M. Romero, and F. Wu. 2008. Crowdsourcing, Attention and Productivity, *arXiv:0809.3030v1* (2008).

Huberman, B.A., and L. Adamic. 2004. Information dynamics in the networked world. In *Complex Networks*, edited by E. Ben-Naim, H. Frauenfelder, and Z. Toroczkai, eds., 371-395. Springer.

Huberman, B. A. 2002. *The Laws of the Web: Patterns in the Ecology of Information*. Cambridge, Mass.: MIT Press.

Huberman, B. A., P. L. T. Pirolli, J. E. Pitkow, and R. M. Lukose. 1998. Strong Regularities in World Wide Web Surfing. *Science* 280 (5360): 95–97.

Kempe, D., J. Kleinberg, and E. Tardos. 2003. Maximizing the Spread of Influence through a Social Network. *Proceedings of the Ninth ACM International Conference on Knowledge Discovery and Data Mining*, Washington, D. C., August 24-27, 2003. Klamer, A., and H. P. Van Dalen. 2002. Attention and the Art of Scientific Publishing. *Journal of Economic Methodology* 9: 289–315.

Lanham, Richard. 2006. *The Economics of Attention: Style and Substance in the Age of Information*. Chicago: University of Chicago Press.

Leskovek, J., L. Adamic, and B. A. Huberman. 2007. The Dynamics of Viral Marketing. *ACM Transactions on the Web* 1(1): 5.

Tyler, J. R., D. M. Wilkinson, and B. A. Huberman. 2003. Email as Spectroscopy: Automated Discovery of Community Structure within Organizations. In *Proceedings of the International Conference on Communities and Technologies*, edited by M. H. Huysman, E. Wenger, and V. Wulf, 81-96. Springer.

Wasserman. S., and K. Faust. 1994. *Social Network Analysis*. Cambridge and New York: Cambridge University Press.

Wu, Fang, and Bernardo A. Huberman. 2007. Novelty and Collective Attention. *Proceedings of National Academy of Sciences* (USA) 104: 17599–17601.

Digital Humanities Centers: Loci for Digital Scholarship

Diane M. Zorich

Over the past decade, digital humanities centers (DHCs) have been a driving force in building an agenda for digital scholarship. An organizational entity that emerged in the 1980s, DHCs have dramatically increased in number with the expanded use of digital technology by humanities scholars. Today there are dozens of centers in U.S. universities and research institutes. Although DHCs vary in size and activities, and some have more robust funding, staffing, and scope than others, collectively they may be characterized as entities where new media and technologies are used for humanities-based research, teaching, and intellectual engagement and experimentation. Their goal is to further humanities scholarship, create new forms of knowledge, and explore technology's impact on humanities-based disciplines. In doing so, they offer scholars a unique environment for extending the boundaries of traditional research using digital technologies.

Our Cultural Commonwealth, the seminal 2006 American Council of Learned Societies (ACLS) report that cogently outlines the necessary components for a humanities and social studies cyberinfrastructure, calls for a network of national centers to provide environments that facilitate collaboration, support innovation, cultivate leadership, and encourage digital scholarship. In the absence of such a network, many of the independent, institutionally based DHCs have been working hard to provide such environments at the local level, allowing humanists to address important, nascent issues in digital scholarship.

What can we learn from the experience of DHCs as we look beyond independent, local efforts toward the creation of a network that supports large-scale work across the humanities?

Along with the notable achievements of DHCs, summarized in the pages that follow, come concerns that the proliferation of independent centers is creating silos of activity and redundant resources. There are worries about the prodigious amounts of digital production created by DHCs that remain untethered to larger, community-wide resources and preservation efforts. And there is a sense that center-based research agendas are at odds with digital scholarship's increasing need for large-scale collaborative endeavors and resource integration across departmental, disciplinary, and geographic lines. As the centers mature and their numbers increase, these concerns raise questions about whether DHCs are inadvertently hindering the very research landscape they seek to advance.

This paper, which draws on a study conducted for the Council on Library and Information Resources (CLIR) (Zorich 2008), reviews key accomplishments of DHCs, while also identifying the limitations of current models for a national infrastructure.

The Current State of Play

A survey of 32 DHCs conducted for the CLIR study describes the nature and characteristics of these centers and their maturation from singular projects to multitiered programs. Survey results suggest that DHCs can be grouped into two general categories:

1. Center focused: Centers organized around a physical location, with many diverse projects, programs, and activities undertaken by faculty, researchers, and students, and that offer different resources to diverse audiences. Most centers operate under this model.
2. Resource focused: Centers organized around a primary resource, located in a virtual space, that serve a specific group of individuals. All programs and products flow from the resource, and individuals and institutions help sustain the resource by providing content, labor, or other support services.

Both types of centers have been hubs of activity and experimentation. They are the headquarters for a vast array of digital humanities projects, programs, and events, and they house many of the raw materials—the digital collections and archives—of digital scholarship. While there are increasing calls for shared resources and infrastructure at a level beyond what individual centers can provide, the collective achievements of the surveyed centers are noteworthy, particularly in the following areas.

Transforming humanities scholarship

A common foundation that underlies all DHC mission statements is the desire to transform humanities scholarship. DHCs envision a new type of humanist scholar, one who uses information technology to produce and disseminate humanities research in new ways and to new audiences. The centers have enabled scholars to explore the potential of new technologies to transform scholarship, and have used their many activities to demonstrate how this transformation can occur.

Promoting the enduring value of the humanities in an increasingly digital world

The principles that guide DHCs mirror time-honored beliefs in the humanities, such as faith in humanistic traditions, the importance of the liberal arts, and the conviction that the humanities have a vital contribution to make in the contemporary world. DHCs are promoting and defending these beliefs in the context of the digital domain. For example, the long-held humanistic tradition of open dialog and the free flow of ideas now must include strong support for a progressive intellectual property system that makes this possible in the digital realm. And the humanist mission of developing a citizenry of critical thinkers now must acknowledge the importance of visual and multimedia literacy to achieve this end.

Serving as "sandboxes" and idea incubators

Some DHCs offer a "sandbox"[1] for scholars to explore and test new ideas and technologies in an entrepreneurial environment: they can be a "zone of experimentation and innovation" for humanists.[2] When ideas developed in the sandbox look particularly promising, the centers play an "incubator" role, supporting the ideas and helping accelerate their implementation. In the United States, DHCs have been instrumental in nurturing experimental or experiential activities in digital art and performance, in the changing nature of literacy in a networked culture, and in the re-envisioning of the "publication" in a digital environment. Indeed, some of the most iconic digital humanities research projects, tools, and digital collections were conceived in DHCs.[3]

Eliminating boundaries and fostering interdisciplinarity

DHCs provide an environment where the boundaries of academic departments, disciplines, time, and location can be rendered inconsequential. They cut across the humanities, and the interstitial areas between the humanities, the social and natural sciences, the arts, and technology, to pursue their individual research agendas. Many centers create this climate in a "brick and mortar" environment by bringing scholars from different fields together in a physical location, but a small number also render it virtually, via a collaboratory model in which researchers and scholars pursue a research agenda in exclusively virtual environments.[4]

---

[1] A term borrowed from the software-development industry to describe a space where programmers can create new software functions and test their codes without risk to essential systems.

[2] James O'Donnell, provost at Georgetown University, used this phrase at an ACLS Commission on Cyberinfrastructure Public Information Gathering session to describe an unquantifiable, albeit critical, aspect of digital humanities centers.

[3] For example, *The Valley of the Shadow* project, developed at the Institute for Advanced Studies in the Humanities at the University of Virginia; Zotero, a research tool developed at the Center for History and New Media at George Mason University; and the *Willa Cather Archive*, developed at the Center for Digital Research in the Humanities at the University of Nebraska-Lincoln.

[4] Cf. HASTAC (http://www.hastac.org/) or MERLOT (http://www.merlot.org/merlot/index.htm).

Extending audiences for humanities scholarship

By aggressively harnessing digital distribution channels, some DHCs strive to democratize and revitalize the humanities for diverse audiences. Their constituencies go beyond academe's triumvirate of researcher / scholar / student to include K–12 communities,[5] business and industry,[6] government and community groups,[7] and the general public. It is not unusual for a center to work with local schools to integrate digital history collections into classroom programs,[8] or to invite the general public to contribute content to a digital archive.[9] These and other efforts are extending the humanities to a wider range of audiences.

Engaging a broad community of professionals

DHCs recognize that digital scholarship requires the engagement of a broader network of professionals than does traditional scholarship. To that end, many DHCs have brought on board (as staff, consultants, or partners) an array of experts from many different fields. Librarians, archivists, and museum professionals, who have always played an important but understated role in overseeing scholarly research collections, may be sought out for their expertise in areas such as collections information management and metadata creation. Computer scientists and engineers are enlisted in efforts to develop computational tools for analyzing large data sets or creating data visualizations. Artists and performers, who are often pioneers in creating new forms of expression and interpretation, may be sought for projects that explore novel modes of interpretation and knowledge creation.

Providing a digital humanities training ground

DHCs have served as a de facto training ground for the next generation of digital humanities researchers and scholars. They not only offer conventional educational programs (courses, internships, seminars, and workshops) but also cultivate and nurture leaders in this arena through fellowships and residency programs. Their directors and senior staff mentor graduate and undergraduate students, as well as professionals in the early stages of their careers. Individuals who work and train in the centers are attractive candidates for digital humanities positions at other colleges and universities.

---

5 For example, *Civics Online*, a project of MATRIX—The Center for Humane Arts, Letters & Social Sciences to help K–12 teachers teach civics (http://www.civics-online.org/).

6 See *Human Tech*, an affiliates program for industry offered by the Stanford Humanities Lab (http://www.stanford.edu/group/shl/cgi-bin/drupal/?q=node/1).

7 See the *Scotts Run Writing Heritage Project*, an effort between the Center for Literary Computing at West Virginia University and the Scotts Run community to document the history of a community settlement house (http://www.as.wvu.edu/~srsh/).

8 For example, the Center for Digital History at the University of Virginia incorporates digital history collections into Virginia's K–12 history curricula (http://www.vcdh.virginia.edu/index.php?page=VCDH).

9 Consider, for example, what the Center for History and New Media did with its *September 11 Archive* and its *Hurricane Digital Memory Bank* projects (http://chnm.gmu.edu/collecting-and-exhibiting).

Realizing that humanities computing is an important skill, traditional humanities departments are adding digital humanities coursework to their degree requirements. Because these departments usually lack the resident expertise needed to develop and teach these courses, some rely on DHCs to assist them in this effort. In response, DHCs are creating new courses in digital scholarship and expanding existing offerings on the use of digital technology within specific humanities disciplines. As the demand for digital humanities training continues to grow, some DHCs, in concert with other academic departments, are developing formal degree programs in this area. They are also developing internships, residencies, and postdoctoral fellowships to round out their offerings.

Leading pedagogical innovation

Centers often are on the forefront of innovative teaching and instructional methods for learning in the humanities. They are building rich digital teaching environments (akin to what Stephen Murray has accomplished with *Mapping Gothic France*) and are teaching in virtual worlds. Some DHCs develop innovative techniques within a specific disciplinary area (for example, in the teaching of art, languages, or history) while others explore aspects of pedagogy in the digital arena (such as writing and literacy in new media environments).[10]

The success of DHCs in creatively using technologies for teaching and learning has been recognized beyond the humanities sphere. University administrators see the efforts of DHCs to incorporate digital humanities into liberal arts curricula as reinvigorating the humanities across the university. Educators recognize that DHCs are helping bring information literacy to undergraduate education. And teachers (from the higher education community through K–12) have praised the transformational learning experiences that DHCs bring to their classrooms.

Building collaborations

Digital humanities is an inherently collaborative endeavor, and DHCs have established many collaborations that promote scholarship and community building in various research areas. Collaborators include national and international partners from every imaginable community: higher education and K–12, community groups and cultural organizations, governmental and nongovernmental agencies, broadcast and print media, foundations and funding agencies, and more. Among these collaborators is an eclectic mix of professionals who have been brought into the research fold, such as information managers, engineers, and publishers.

Because of this bank of experience, many directors of DHCs are aware of the elements needed to ensure successful collaborations with diverse partners. However, their collaborative endeavors tend to be small and narrowly focused, addressing the attributes of

10 For examples, see the efforts of WIDE (Writing in Digital Environments) at http://www.wide.msu.edu/projects, and *Rome Reborn* (http://www.romereborn.virginia.edu/), a project at the Institute for Advanced Technology in the Humanities, University of Virginia.

partners and processes but not the nature of the collaborative work. Their parochial focus puts into question whether DHC collaborations can scale up to meet the complex management, interactions, and communications required for more broad-based, community-wide research needs.

Enhancing the scholarly research process

DHCs have developed an array of products that support and promote digital scholarship. The most visible of these are tools for publishing research and organizing and analyzing data. There have been unquestionable successes in this area (as evidenced by tools such as Zotero, Omeka, and Sophie[11]), but there are also concerns that DHC tools are inadequately leveraged across the humanities. Many tools are under-resourced, poorly maintained, and not widely known outside of a particular center. New efforts are under way to scrutinize DHC tool development and address some of these problems community-wide.[12]

DHCs also develop digital collections and resources (such as online repositories of learning materials or digital archives of humanities texts) that make the source materials of research more accessible for study and computational analysis. They create digital workspaces (such as wikis and blogs) and publication venues (e-journals and e-newsletters) for collaborating on projects and sharing news and research results, and they use virtual worlds to demonstrate artwork and performances. To distribute humanities resources more broadly, they develop products (such as virtual exhibits, podcasts, and Webcasts) designed to reach large audiences, and create special utilities (plug-ins, desktop versions of digital libraries, PDF documents) that allow research to be conducted on the scholar's local desktop. This rich array of digital resources is a double-edged sword: they provide the raw material for new research, but few DHCs have preservation plans and digital repositories to enable greater exposure and long-term access to these materials. Consequently, much of this digital production risks being orphaned, rendered obsolete, or limited to the environs of the particular DHC in which it was created.

On the programmatic side, DHCs have developed and fostered long-term efforts that incorporate many singular activities for the purposes of a larger scholarly objective. For example, they may sponsor complex projects and experiments that explore the use of three-dimensional modeling techniques for the re-creation of an archaeological site. Or they may work on multitiered programs to explore broader issues such as preserving virtual worlds. By developing or hosting programs (rather than one-off projects), DHCs commit long-term resources to various research areas. But here, too, the silo-like nature of DHCs poses a problem: the research agendas and activities of centers often overlap, resulting in redundant efforts and the unwise use of resources.

---

[11] See Zotero at http://www.zotero.org/; Omeka at http://omeka.org/; and Sophie at http://www.sophieproject.org/.

[12] See Nguyen and Shilton 2008; and Project Bamboo at http://projectbamboo.org/.

Providing operational services to the scholarly community

One aspect of digital scholarship that receives scant consideration is the operational support that allows such scholarship to flourish. Because other campus units do not readily offer this support, DHCs have stepped in to fill the void.

DHCs' operational support comes in many forms. In the area of technical infrastructure, DHCs provide technology for scholars conducting field research, build and maintain hardware/software infrastructure for online communities, and design and create digital laboratory environments. They provide Internet services in the form of Web hosting, storage space, and site mirroring, and offer scholars and organizations server space for archiving inactive projects, workspaces, and image, audio, or video files.

DHCs also offer technical assistance and expertise in areas such as metadata encoding, digital resource design, statistical analysis, hardware/software support, media digitization, and technology prototyping. In the pedagogical arena, some centers train both new and established scholars in instructional design methods for humanities courses, and assist teachers with introducing curricula that incorporate technology into their classrooms. They also manage language lab facilities and new media classrooms.

Other forms of operational support come in the guise of management and administration services such as project planning, brokering services, office assistance, and grant administration. DHCs may also provide a temporary home base for related organizations and groups that have not yet secured an independent footing or are in a transitional state.

A less tangible mode of support comes in the form of advisory activity. Respected for their experience, DHC staff members are often asked to consult with academic, cultural, nonprofit, government, and corporate entities on a range of humanities and digitization issues. They are tapped by leaders in industry, government, and the media for their insights on national trends, current best practices, and particular high-profile projects. Funding agencies request their assistance with peer review of digital humanities projects, and academic tenure-and-promotion committees seek their advice when reviewing faculty members engaged in digital humanities research.

The Role of DHCs in Promoting Digital Scholarship

As noted earlier, the independent nature of DHCs has given rise to several concerns. These include overlapping agendas and activities, which create redundancies that inefficiently use scarce resources in the humanities community; the balkanization of DHCs from traditional humanities departments, to the detriment of humanities scholarship as a whole (SCI 2008, 14); and a lack of the large-scale, coordinated efforts needed to build a humanities cyberinfrastructure and address marquee research issues.

These concerns have led to a rethinking of the nature and form of DHCs and to discussions of how they can "complement each other and constitute a whole greater than the sum of its parts" (SCI 2008, 3). Scholars now are asking how centers can be positioned to bring about desired large-scale change that will transform teaching, research, and scholarship *across* the humanities. Some suggestions include aligning centers that have complementary strengths, and forming alliances between centers to fill knowledge gaps (SCI 2008, 3). The idea of regional or national centers has been proposed to leverage resources, cast a wider net of support for the community, and support large-scale collaborative projects (ACLS 2006, 35).

Whatever prospects are envisioned, the current landscape requires greater clarity about the roles for different types of centers (e.g., local, regional or national, resource based), as well as strategies for inclusion and interaction between them. It also requires consideration of the nature of collaborative work. A recent study of more than 200 scientific collaboratories suggests that large-scale collaborations are most successful when the work is easily divided into components rather than "tightly coupled" (Bos et al. 2004). Findings also show that collaborations organized around the sharing of data or tools are more successful than those organized around the sharing of knowledge, and that projects involving aggregation of resources are easier to develop than projects involving co-creation of resources (Bos et al. 2007). These findings suggest that with respect to promoting digital scholarship, the nature of the collaborative work is as important as the type of center where that work is conducted.

As scholars ponder how to promote digital scholarship in the humanities, many believe the term "digital scholarship" is destined for obsolescence. They argue that the distinction between "scholarship" and "digital scholarship" becomes meaningless as research and cultural production increasingly occur in a digital realm. A similar argument might be made about DHCs as distinct entities in the humanities landscape. While they now support new forms of scholarly creativity and production, they may become outmoded—viewed as places that helped bridge the divide between traditional and digital scholarship, or as precursors to a yet-to-be developed scholarly research environment (much like *Wunderkammern* are precursors of modern museums).

Whatever scenario evolves, today's DHCs are, individually and collectively, facing barriers such as siloing, redundancies, and non-integrated digital production that limit their effectiveness in meeting the current needs of digital scholarship. Nevertheless, they remain focal points in their respective institutions for digital humanities research and teaching, and have been critical in moving the process and products of scholarship into the digital arena. Their insights and expertise make them important voices in discussions on how to move digital scholarship forward.

References

American Council of Learned Societies Commission on Cyberinfrastructure for the Humanities and Social Sciences. 2006. *Our Cultural Commonwealth*. New York: American Council of Learned Societies. Available at http://www.acls.org/uploadedFiles/Publications/Programs/Our_Cultural_Commonwealth.pdf.

Bos, Nathan, Ann Zimmerman, Judith Olson, Jude Yew, Jason Yerkie, Erik Dahl, and Gary Olson. 2007. From Shared Databases to Communities of Practice: A Taxonomy of Collaboratories. *Journal of Computer-Mediated Communication* 12(2). Available at http://jcmc.indiana.edu/vol12/issue2/bos.html.

Bos, Nathan, Erik Hofer, and Judy Olson. 2004. How Are Public Data Contributions Rewarded in Open Genetics Databases? Paper presented at the Science of Collaboratories Symposium, New Orleans, LA, August 6–12, 2004. PowerPoint presentation available at http://www.scienceofcollaboratories.org/NewsEvents/AOM/Bos_PublicData.ppt

Nguyen, Lilly, and Katie Shilton. 2008. CLIR Tools for Humanists Project. Appendix F in Zorich, Diane M.: *A Survey of Digital Humanities Centers in the United States*. Washington, DC: Council on Library and Information Resources; 57-58.

Scholarly Communication Institute. 2008. Introduction and Summary. Scholarly Communication Institute 6: Humanities Research Centers. University of Virginia, Charlottesville, VA, July 13–15, 2008. Available at http://www.uvasci.org/wp-content/uploads/2008/09/sci-6-report.pdf.

Zorich, Diane M. 2008. *A Survey of Digital Humanities Centers in the United States*. Washington, DC: Council on Library and Information Resources. Available at http://www.clir.org/pubs/abstract/pub143abst.html.